Tales of a Pioneer Journalist

**From Gold Rush to Government Street
in 19th Century Victoria**

by

David Williams Higgins

Selected chapters from
The Mystic Spring and The Passing of a Race,
two books written by D.W. Higgins
over 90 years ago

Heritage House

PHOTO CREDITS

B.C. Provincial Archives: Pages 26, 36, 60, 76, 91, 106, 115,
122, 130, 133, 147, 154, 187, 190.
Manitoba Archives: Page 80
Vancouver Public Library: Pages 6, 174-75, 177.
All other photos from Heritage House Collection.

Canadian Cataloguing in Publication Data
Higgins, David Williams, 1834-1917
   Tales of a Pioneer Journalist

Selection of chapters from the author's The passing of a race and The mystic spring.

ISBN 1-895811-24-4

   1. Higgins, David Williams, 1834-1917.   2. Fraser River Valley (B.C.)--
Gold discoveries.   3. Gold miners--British Columbia--Biography.
I. Title.   II. Title: The passing of a race.   III. Title: The mystic spring.
FC3822.4.H53 1995   971.1'02'092   C94-910295-4
F1089.F7H53 1995

First Edition – 1996

Edited by Art Downs
Cover Design by Cecilia Hirczy Welsford

HERITAGE HOUSE PUBLISHING COMPANY LTD.
Unit #8 – 17921 55th Ave., Surrey B.C., V3S 6C4

Printed in Canada

Contents

The Author 4

The Golden Wedding 8

A Child that Found Its Father 19

The Farewell Banquet 31

My First Christmas Dinner in Victoria, 1860 35

An Ill-fated Family 47

The Saint and the Sinner 55

Why B.C. Lost the San Juan Islands 64

The Mayorial Banquet—or Brawl? 70

The Dual 79

Fate Was the Hunter 88

Jem McLaughlin's Transformation 96

Sweet Marie 103

B.C.'s Worst Marine Disaster 114

The Passing of a Race 124

The John Bright Massacre 132

A Fugitive from Justice 136

The Wrong Saddlebags 146

A Queer Character 157

Lost in the Mountains on Christmas Day 161

The Pork-Pie Hat 167

The Lions 176

Happy Tom 184

THE AUTHOR

David William Higgins arrived at Fort Victoria on Vancouver Island in 1858. He was among the first of some 30,000 men stampeding to a gold rush on a little-known river called the

Fraser. Like virtually all other stampeders, however, he discovered that placer mining involved a maximum of work for a minimum of gold. But unlike most of the newcomers who left by autumn, he remained in B.C. all of his life, becoming one of the province's best known pioneer residents.

Higgins was born in Halifax in 1834 but was brought up in Brooklyn where he served an apprenticeship as a printer. In 1852 he journeyed to California, hoping to become wealthy in the California gold field. But that rush was over and, instead of mining, he joined the *San Francisco Morning Call* as editor and part owner. In 1858 he sold his interest and headed north "...in a mad rush to the British possessions on the Pacific in search of gold."

When he arrived on the Fraser River all productive ground was staked so he bought an interest in a claim in front of Fort Yale — today's Yale. To support himself he took charge of Ballou's Express office in Yale and became a correspondent for several California newspapers. His first-hand descriptions are today a treasure of information about the Fraser River stampede and B.C.'s pioneer era. In 1860 he left Yale for Victoria where he joined the staff of the *Colonist* newspaper and eventually became the owner. The paper, now nearing 150 years old, is still published as the *Victoria Times-Colonist*.

In addition to a distinguished newspaper career, Higgins was active in community affairs. He was a sponsor of Victoria's first fire department and theatre, and became president of the National Electric Tramway and Lighting Company. In 1886 he was elected to the provincial legislature, then four years later

Fort Victoria prior to the 1858 gold-rush stampede. At the time the Hudson's Bay Company leased all of Vancouver Island from the British Government for $1.50 a year.

The vessel is the historic *Beaver*, built for the Hudson's Bay Company. She arrived in 1835 via Cape Horn, the first steam vessel on the coast of North and South America. She served for over 50 years, finally being wrecked at the entrance to Vancouver harbour in 1888.

B.C.'s first parliament buildings that the author knew so well. Built between 1858-1862, their unusual architectural style resulted in them becoming known as the "Birdcages."

Below: The new parliament buildings nearing completion in 1897, one of the birdcages in the foreground. The new buildings opened in 1898, with one birdcage surviving until 1957 when it burned down.

became speaker of the Legislative Assembly. He served with distinction for nine years, then resigned. Three years later he retired from public life, although his active mind wouldn't let him simply fade away. He wrote two books, *The Mystic Spring* and *The Passing of a Race.* This book is a selection from them, some stories edited slightly for length and style.

Of his books, Higgins noted:

"My opportunities for collecting material have been excellent, for I have had a strangely adventurous and variant career. I have prospected, mined and traded; owned a theatre and managed theatrical companies; filled every position in a newspaper office from 'devil' to editor and proprietor; and have been a politician and legislator, rounding off my public career by resignation after presiding as Speaker for nine years over the British Columbia Legislature.

"During the half century that I was in active life I made copious notes of events as they transpired. I carefully studied the peculiarities of speech, the habits and mode of life, and the frailties, as well as the virtues, of the early gold-seekers on the Pacific Coast and now venture to lay some of the most startling incidents that came to my knowledge before the reading public.

"The reminiscent stories are all founded upon actual occurrences, and in the years to come may be found of value to the student of early events in California and the British Pacific. I have aimed to write history, so far as it came under my own observation, in an entertaining manner. How far I have succeeded I leave to the judgment of the reader."

Higgins died in 1917 at 83. In addition to his two books and tens of thousands of words about the province's pioneer people and events, Higgins left another memorial of the pre-1900s era. In 1885 in Victoria he had built one of the city's finest homes. Called Regent's Park House, it included seventeen rooms, eight fireplaces and a grand staircase.

Fortunately, it has survived. Today it is an offical Heritage House, open to the public, and a bridge back to the province's gold-rush era that Higgins knew so well.

The Golden Wedding

The fledgling community of Victoria had never seen anything like the gold-miner's wedding — and over 130 years later has still never seen its equal.

The fall of 1862 witnessed the return from Cariboo of a large number of miners with heavy swags of gold dust, and Victoria was the scene of many uproarious gatherings. The owners of the Abbott, Point, Diller, Steele, Barker, Adams, Cameron and other very rich claims on Williams Creek congregated here and seemed to find difficulty in getting rid of their money.

A story is told of Abbott, chief owner of the Abbott claim, from which gold was washed by the bucketful for many weeks. Abbott had fished for a living at Fraser mouth before he went to Cariboo and was a very poor man indeed when he settled on the piece of mining ground which afterwards bore his name. He was an easy mark for the gamblers who infested the mining section. He played high and lost with unvarying good nature. He was known to have wagered $5,000 on a single poker hand. Having lost, he appeared the following night with another big sum which he sent hurtling down the table in search of that which had gone before — sending good money after bad, as the saying is. Abbott, with a number of friends, entered the St. James Hotel bar one evening and called for drinks for the crowd. Having been served he asked what the mirror behind the bar was worth.

"Forty dollars," replied the barkeeper.

Taking a number of nuggets from his pocket, Abbott discharged them full at the glass, breaking it into many pieces.

"Take its value out of that and keep the change," he said, as he left the place. The nuggets were sold at the express office for a figure exceeding $100.

A few of these yarn-swapping retired miners likely attended the Golden Wedding. Years later they pose on Main Street outside the Angel Hotel. Below: The short-lived St. James Club rented space near the Hudson's Bay Company fort until the wedding fiasco.

The next day nearly all the bars in town were equipped with large mirrors in the hope that Abbott or some other suddenly-made-rich fool would break and pay for them as had been done with the glass at St. James. But Abbott had gone out of the looking-glass business, for he broke no more, and none of his friends followed his silly example.

Early in the year there had arrived from London a Mr. and Mrs. Shoolber. They brought with them a complete and valuable stock of dry goods, furs, mantles and millinery which had been selected from the wholesale stock of a very extensive dry goods firm in London, whose chief partner was father of Mr. Shoolber. In addition to the stock, the Shoolbers brought with them a young servant girl or "slavey," as well as a milliner, a dressmaker and a saleswoman.

Now it so happened that the milliner and dressmaker, being attractive persons, were shortly wooed and won by two of the rich miners. As they were under contract with the firm for a year, to avoid legal complications they skipped off to the U.S. and were married and remained there. The saleswoman, being rather plain, did not attract as many admirers. But one day a miner known as Bill Lovidge made up to her and proposed matrimony. After a two hours' courtship the pair became engaged.

Mrs. Shoolber was inconsolable when the news was broken to her. She had paid for the passages of all three out and, before they had been here a month, two were gone and the other was preparing to go. She appealed to Mr. Lovidge as a gentleman of honor not to take a mean advantage of the firm, but to wait until the expiration of a year before marrying the woman. But Bill was obdurate. He wanted to get married and he wanted to get married right away.

What was the pecuniary value the firm placed on the services of the woman for the next ten months? A trifle of $1,000 was named. Pshaw! that was a mere fleabite. He would pay it. But there were the passage money and sundry other expenses, amounting to say, $500. That would be all right. Mr. Lovidge would pay them, too. Then there was a trousseau. A final clause in the agreement under which the girl would be given her liberty must be that Mrs. Shoolber should have the providing of the bride's wedding outfit. How much would that amount to? Well, another bagatelle of $1,000, not to exceed that — making $2,500 in all. "A mere nothing," quoth Bill. "Prepare a demand note and I'll sign it." This being done the work of preparation went rapidly and gaily forward. When it came to providing clothes for the prospective bridegroom, Mrs. Shoolber recommended Goldstein & Co., who had a tailoring establishment. I presume that she got what is termed a "rake-off," because she guaranteed the account, which ran up into the hundreds, for both firms just laid on their charges as with a trowel. The Shoolbers were friends of three men who owned the St. James Club — had known them in London — so to them was assigned the task of preparing a banquet. They were directed to spare no expense in providing for one hundred guests.

At the end of two weeks the preparations were complete. The bride had tried on her gowns and hats and hoops, and they were pronounced perfect dreams. The happy man had been fitted with his wedding garments, to his own satisfaction if not that of his friends. The foray on the henneries and pigsties had been so complete that not a cock crew, a hen cackled, a chicken peeped, a duck quacked or a sucking pig squealed within five miles of Victoria — all having been requisitioned for the Lovidge wedding feast. A free hand had been given the caterers and Mrs. Shoolber in the matter of invitations. As it was in their interest to have lots of food and drink consumed, about one hundred persons were asked.

When the evening at last arrived the dining hall was crowded with all classes and conditions of men and a dozen or so women. The table decorations were superb. There were few flowers, but there were many tiny flags. Suspended on colored cords from the ceiling were numerous tin angels and cupids in short dresses, in various attitudes of flight, with expanded wings and fat legs that seemed too big for the bodies. There were fairy lamps and wax candles flaring merrily away. Here and there on the board were sprigs of evergreen in earthern pots that in the end got sadly mixed up with floating island, boned turkey and corned beef, young pigs, and sundry fat geese.

The banquet was announced for seven o'clock, but it was eight before the dinner appeared. Meanwhile, the guests had been industriously filling their empty stomachs with wine, beer and whiskey. When at last they sat down, amid much confusion, laughing and loud talking, many of the number were decidedly "fu'." The eatables were dumped on the tables all at once, as it were, leaving the guests to make their selections after the manner in which goods are chosen at a bargain counter.

Some of the ladies wore dresses low-cut in front and behind, and others wore high waists that reached nearly to their ears. Before the bride and groom appeared the half-famished guests had fallen foul of the food. There was a plenitude of knives and forks, but spoons were shy, so when some of the guests were required to stir the contents of their cups they used the knives and forks in preference to their index fingers. When Bill Lovidge and his wife entered some stood up and cheered, but most retained their seats, being far gone on the road to inebriety, and contented themselves with calling out "Howyer, Bill?" "Wish you good luck, old feller," "How's yer gal?" and so on.

I shall not attempt a description of the bride's getup, except that it was gorgeous and stunning as a rainbow. But Bill Lovidge — ah! he was arrayed like the lilies of the valley. He wore a tall black hat with a very narrow brim, a light brown sack coat (the tailors complained that he refused to have a coat with tails at any price), a pair of shepherd's plaid trousers, a red vest, a flaring necktie with long ends and a paper collar. His gloves were white and he refused to take them off, persisting in eating with them on, in spite of the remonstrance of his bride.

When he first took his seat he did not uncover, insisting that it was out of fashion to do so. But at last, yielding to the request of one of the hosts, he consented to remove his tall hat placing it carefully by the side of his chair. Here it was slyly kicked and cuffed and buffeted by the waiters as they passed to and fro until it was reduced to a condition of pulp and could never be again worn. To top everything, Lovidge wore eye-glasses, and the patronizing air with which he regarded his guests and fellow-diggers of the mine as he gazed along the tables was too funny to be described. I believe the bride and groom were the only ones at the table who were provided with napkins (Bill had his tucked beneath his chin) and served with soup. As the eye-glasses were a very ill-behaved pair, they had a disagreeable habit of occasionally dropping from the bridge of Bill's nose into the soup. He fished them out with his spoon and, having dried them with the napkin, returned them to their proper resting place. This operation was repeated half a dozen times during the evening until Bill's face wore a fat expression of greasy contentment.

It cannot be denied that the bridegroom was under the influence of the rosy god, and so were nearly all the guests. The supply of drinkables was unlimited. There was plenty of food, but it was badly cooked and worse served and was as cold as ice.

The corps of waiters was very limited, and it was by the greatest good luck that any one who had not the ability to help himself got anything at all. The waiters, too, were suffering from the general complaint. Now and again a great crash would be heard, succeeded by a few smothered oaths, a sound as if a heavy body was being dragged over the floor towards the door, accompanied by a thump! thump! We were told that one of the firm had converted himself into an all round bouncer, and that he was busily employed in looking after the welfare and morals of the unhappy waiters who had taken too much by kicking them out of the room.

The sound of revelry by night that Byron wrote about would have been dead silence if placed by the side of the Golden

Wedding banquet at the St. James. I doubt if Wellington would have heard the roar of the opening guns at Waterloo above the din had he been present on the memorable evening.

As the evening wore on I was much amused by a wordy conflict between a Northern and a Southern man as to the merits of his respective section. The U.S. Civil War between the North and South was then on and feeling ran high. From words the men came to blows. In their struggle they fell across the table, shattering crockery and glassware and upsetting food and wine. The women screamed.

One fainted and did not revive until one of the male guests proposed to dash a goblet of water in her face. Another produced a snuff-box and insisted upon giving her a pinch. A third wanted to sever her stay laces, which were drawn quite taut, when she suddenly came to, passed a hand dreamily over her face and, after hysterically demanding to be told where she was, resumed her place at the table. Meanwhile, a ring had been formed about the belligerents, and the late Ned Allen, afterwards Member of Parliament for Lillooet, who had done a little pugilism in his day in England, undertook to act as umpire.

As fate would have it, while nearly all the guests wore sack coats, and some who had no sacks appeared in their overcoats, those who had neither came in the miner's ordinary gray shirt with a pistol belt (minus the pistol) around their waists to keep up their trousers. One of the combatants, the Northern man, had on the only dress coat in the room. He was the pride of the occasion — the pink of fashion and the mould of form. Amid that singularly arrayed company, the clawhammer coat of the Northern man stood out in bold relief like a storm signal against a cloudy sky or a game cock on top of a fence hurling defiance at the sultan of a neighboring barnyard.

The other male guests felt that they were at a disadvantage. The wearer was the Beau Brummel of the evening. It was true that the rest of his apparel did not conform with the coat, for he wore a pair of H.B. Company's corduroys. He had the coat buttoned up as far as the buttons went, but peeping out from behind the lapels was the vision of a "biled" shirt! These two innovations proved his ruin. The clawhammer coat or the "biled" shirt might have been condoned had they stood alone, but the two together were a combination not to be borne by a company such as had assembled in honor of the distinguished bride and bridegroom.

That the ladies rejoiced that there was one gentleman in the room who had been well bred and had been somewhere before was evidenced by the approving glances they shot at him. Every little while a lady would raise her glass and, calling the dress

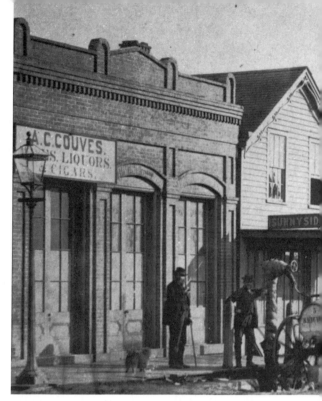

Government Street in Victoria in the early 1860s, a jumble of mostly wooden buildings fronting onto uneven sidewalks and dirt streets. Water was delivered by horse-drawn wagons at up to 25 cents a bucket.

coat wearer by name, would exclaim, "I looks tovards you." The gentleman would rise in all the magnificence of his fashionable apparel, place his hand on his heart and reply as he drained his glass, "I likevise bows."

"The h'only person dressed like a gentleman at this table," remarked one belle, as she conveyed a piece of cold ham to her mouth on the blade of her knife. "I should like to be hintroducted."

Another fair one was heard to remark, "He puts me in mind so much of a 'andsome gentleman I met at 'ome the last time I dined at the dook's."

I was greatly amused by an exchange between two ladies who occupied seats on opposite sides of the table. Said one, speaking across the board, and referring to him of the clawhammer:

"That's Mr. Perkins, of Barkerville, ain't it?"

"Yes," said the other, "that's him. My! Don't he look fine!"

"Indeed he do. He's quite 'caffee or lay!'"

"Wh-a-at?" returned the other. "You means 'oh! fat' (*au fait* she intended to say, I thought), don't you?"

"I means just what I said — 'caffee or lay,' " she glared back. " 'Oh! Fat,' indeed! Do you want to insult him?"

"Why, what you said means coffee and cream."

14

"When I went to school it meant that a person was just the thing — that he was all there," was the scornful retort.

"Oh!" retorted the friend, sarcastically, "Parley voo Frankay?"

"No, thank you," snorted the other with indignation, "I never use Chinook in company — only low people does that."

"Person!" cried the lady on the opposite side.

"Woman!" was tossed back with a hiss.

"Oh! oh!" screamed the other. "She called me a woman! Take me away. Some one lead me off to bed. I cannot bear the sight of that hugly face no more." She threw herself back in the chair and commenced to beat a sort of devil's tattoo on the floor with the heels of her shoes, while she wept and laughed by turns.

"Highstericks," exclaimed one of the waiters who rushed on the scene. "Here, some one take off her shoes and stockings and spank the soles of her feet hard with your bare hands. That'll bring her to. My sister used to have them fits, and that's the way we used to cure her."

Someone made a move to follow the instructions thus given and actually removed the shoes. But before the stockings could be taken off, the patient sprang to her feet and walked to the door with the shoes in her hand, sobbing as she went, "She called me a wo-woman!"

Her late antagonist fanned herself violently and beamed affectionately on Mr. Perkins of Barkerville and his tail-coat. All these things had not been lost on the other guests, who were thrown into the shade by the brilliant get-up of the Northern man. I have not the slightest doubt that the fight was pre-arranged with the object of taking the beau of the evening down a peg or two. Under the guidance of Allen the parties clinched, and were struggling and panting with excitement when suddenly a tearing sound like the ripping of a crosscut saw through a thin plank was heard.

The Northern man uttered a sharp cry as he dropped his antagonist. Placing his hands behind him, he discovered that his precious garment had been ripped from waist to shoulders and flapped loosely on either side with naught but the collar and the arms to keep it from an absolute divorce. The sight was too funny for anything. The whole company broke into hysterics of laughter. Men threw themselves on the floor and rolled over and over in their hilarity. The Southern man jumped up and down and cracked his heels in his glee, while the wretched victim made frantic efforts to draw the tails together. All in vain.

The laughter grew louder and more pronounced when through the rent it was seen that the supposed "biled" (or dress) shirt was only a dickie, or false bosom, held in position by tapes that were tied about the man's body, and that beneath the rent was revealed the victim's underwear! The poor fellow turned round and round in pursuit of his divided skirts like a revolving figure in a show window. But the tails kept ever one lap ahead, until, falling behind hopelessly in the race, he paused and, glaring across at his late antagonist, who was pounding the table in his mirth, shouted: "Durn you, Bill Savage, if it hadn't a-been for you this ere thing wouldn't have occurred. Wait till I catch you outside!"

"Bah!" retorted Savage. "Joe Perkins, it jest serves yer right. If yer hadn't a-put on frills an' airs, and made believe yer was somebody, like the man in the Holy Scriptur', when everybody knows yer ain't nobody at all, yer wouldn't have bin rigged out like a scarecrow and come here to lord it over us fellers. It just serves yer right."

There was a murmur of approval, in which the women joined. The other fellow, finding that he had been deposed as a swell and exposed as a fashionable fraud, broke through the yelling crowd and vanished out of the door, his split coat waving its tails in front of him as he went.

The scene was the funniest I ever witnessed in real life. No comedy was ever so ludicrous. I cannot recall in all my experience (and I have a keen sense of the ridiculous) a more laughable picture than that presented by the unfortunate man as he left the dining hall a baffled and betrayed person. He sought the silence of the streets and the midnight air to reflect upon his blighted career as a ladies' man — and to lay for Bill Savage.

The wild revel went on and the fun continued fast and furious till long after midnight. More than one of the guests disappeared under the table or left for home. Lovidge still held his own, in spite of the expostulations and entreaties of his wife, who was rather a nice little body and hadn't touched a drop all evening. But William, who was obstinate, was not disposed to leave while there was any liquor remaining to be drunk.

The St. James people were also interested in opening as many bottles as possible, for the more wine disposed of the larger their bill would be. Among the goodies that occupied space on the dining table was a huge rice pudding. About one-half had been eaten and the remainder, which closely resembled a broken cart wheel thickly encrusted with mud, sat patiently awaiting events in the pan in which it had been baked. No one would have imagined that out of so innocent a thing as a rice pudding an event which wrecked a Golden Wedding would grow.

About two o'clock Bill Lovidge consented to be led or dragged to the nuptial chamber. Two of his Cariboo friends took each an arm and the tearful spouse, with the crushed hat in her hand, followed. It had been arranged to speed the departing couple with a shower of rice, and many of the guests had filled their pockets with the grain and threw it in great handfuls upon the pair as they prepared to leave. One of the guests, who had failed to provide himself with rice, looked about for a substitute. It was Bill Savage.

In an evil moment his eye alighted on the dish containing the remains of the rice pudding. With Savage, to conceive was to execute, and in an instant he had plunged both hands into the soft, yielding mass and hurled it straight at the receding pair. It fell in great pasty patches upon the heads and clothes of Lovidge and his bride and smeared their friends as well. In a moment there was great excitement. Savage was pitched upon by the indignant quartette and a number of the guests and kicked from the room, where he fell into Perkins' hands and was most unmercifully mauled. Others became entangled in the row and a free fight was in progress when the police appeared and dispersed the party.

So ended the Golden Wedding. I know I shall be reminded that the popular idea of a golden wedding is the celebration of the fiftieth anniversary of the nuptials of a couple. Having passed through the joys of honeymoon and survived the storms and temptations of wedded life extending over a half century, they assemble their friends and receive their congratulations and presents as tokens of esteem and love. The picture I have pen-painted is not of the adventures of a pair who had been married for fifty years, but of a couple who had been married scarcely as many minutes when their friends came together and celebrated their union in one of the maddest, wildest and funniest festivals in which it has ever been my lot to take part.

Why was it called a Golden Wedding? Because Bill Lovidge was falsely represented, as "Big Larry" put it, as "rowlin' in gowld," and because his mining friends had related far and near that he was the owner of the richest claim and that he was the wealthiest man in Cariboo.

The banquet and the strange doings thereat were the gossip of the town on the next and many following days. The bills that came pouring in to the newly married man were enormous. Every one had charged his own price for everything. The strangest part of the story is that there was not a dollar available with which to discharge them. The St. James bill was about $1,800. For quick cash the Club offered to accept $1,500. Otherwise the case must go to court. Mrs. Shoolber asked for $3,000, and the tailor's bill and a few casuals brought the total to $5,000 or thereabouts. There was imprisonment for debt here at that time, and while the creditors were preparing to take out writs Lovidge, with the assistance of some of his Cariboo friends, managed to slip away to the American side in a sloop and did not return to Victoria. His wife joined him, and Lovidge, who was a butcher by trade, got employment at San Francisco.

The St. James Club firm came to grief in consequence of the bills they had incurred on account of the Golden Wedding supper. Under the impression that Lovidge was rich, they had joined with Mrs. Shoolber in making the bill as large as possible, and, in common with her, lost everything. The following week the St. James closed its doors and a red flag betokened an auction sale. The Shoolbers suffered a similar fate, and so ends the story.

A Child that Found its Father

During the author's life-long newspaper career he met thousands of people, with George Collins probably the most memorable.

In 1858 there was great excitement along the Pacific Coast upon the discovery of gold on the bars of Fraser River in British Columbia. Miners and business-men from California, Oregon and Washington Territory made their way in thousands to the new gold fields, and the tents of a multitude of gold-seekers lined the banks of that wild stream, while towns and villages sprang up as if by magic. Every available craft was engaged to bear the miners to the Promised Land, and for many weeks steamships, sailing vessels, and even tiny fishing smacks left San Francisco with full lists of passengers and as much freight as could be crammed into their holds. The country washed by the Fraser River was then known as New Caledonia and eventually became part of what is today British Columbia.

In the year mentioned I was a vigorous youth, full of hope and enthusiasm, and left San Francisco for the new gold mines. I built a shack on the townsite of Yale and opened a general store, to which I added the agency of Ballou's Express. I remained at Yale continuously until May 1859, when I had occasion to visit the capital, Victoria, on Vancouver Island. While on my way back on a sternwheel steamer one of the strangest experiences in my life began.

On the first day out I made the acquaintance of a young American who called himself Thomas Eaton. During a close acquaintanceship, which lasted for two years, I found him a thoroughly good chap and perfectly reliable on all occasions. There were several other young fellows on board who were going to try their luck at the new mines. One of these young men was of rather stout build and medium height. He had a refined look, spoke in a slow and guarded manner, and wore his dark hair cut short. The weather was warm, but the evenings were chilly and a top-coat was essential for comfort. This particular young man did not seem to own a top-coat. He wore a long linen duster, and was accustomed to stand on the deck with his hands in his pockets, as if to keep them warm.

"Why don't you put on an overcoat?" I asked him. "You'll catch cold."

"Oh," he shivered back, "I haven't any. I left home in a hurry and forgot to buy one at Victoria." His teeth chattered until I thought they would shake out of their sockets.

"Why don't you get a blanket out of your stateroom and put it over your shoulders?" I asked.

"To tell you the truth," he replied, "I haven't a room or a berth, either."

"But you can get one easily enough," I cried. I called to the purser. "Here's a young man who wants a berth. There's a spare one in my room. There are places for three, and only Eaton and I are in the room."

"All right," said the purser. "The lower berth, is it? Two dollars and a half, please."

"No, no," quickly responded the young fellow. "I couldn't think of inconveniencing you, sir. Two are enough in a room. I'll sit up till we get to Yale tomorrow night. I'm used to sitting up," he continued, "and don't mind it a bit."

The purser, busy man that he was, strode off with an impatient shrug of his shoulders.

"Well, at any rate," said I, "you shall have a covering." So, proceeding to the room, I drew a blanket from the lower bunk and handed it to the young fellow, who accepted it gratefully and put it about him. Then we stood near the smoke stack to enjoy the heat, and exchanged confidences. He told me that his name was Harry Collins, that his father and mother lived at San Francisco, and that he was on his way to join a brother, George Collins, who owned a rich claim somewhere on the Fraser River. About ten o'clock I turned in, leaving Harry Collins standing close as he could to the stack and with the blanket still about him.

In the morning I told Eaton about the young fellow. After breakfast we found him still standing near where I had left him during the night. No, he hadn't slept a wink, and, indeed, his face gave evidence of great fatigue. He looked really ill. Had he breakfasted yet? No, he didn't care for anything to eat. Would a cup of tea or coffee be appreciated?

"No, thank you, I am not thirsty," he said, but in spite of his refusal I thought I noticed a wistful look steal across his face.

Drawing Eaton aside I told him I was afraid that what ailed the young man were pride and poverty. He had no money and was too proud to disclose his plight.

"Let's make him eat," cried Eaton. So together we went to the steward and arranged to have a substantial meal set in the saloon after all the others had left it. Then one of the waiters was sent to Mr. Collins with a message that he was wanted below. All unsuspecting, the young man followed the waiter and the steward told him his breakfast was getting cold.

"But I didn't order breakfast," he exclaimed, starting back.

"Cap'en's orders," returned the steward.

"But — but — I have no money to pay for it," he whispered in the steward's ear.

"You don't have to pay no money for it," replied the steward, who had been duly tipped. "It's all right. This is the Cap'en's birthday, and it's his treat."

Still doubting and protesting, Collins was gently pushed by the steward into a seat, and the waiter asked, "Tea or coffee, sir?"

"Tea, please," he responded. Then, turning to the steward, he said with a suspicious air, "Was no one charged for meals this morning? Was everyone treated the same as I am being treated?"

"Yes," said the wicked steward. "Everybody, and you're the only man that objected. And I'll tell you more; if you don't eat that grub the cap'en will be real mad. He won't take a insult from no one. Did you ever see him mad? No? Well, you don't want to. So you'd better pitch in an' eat before he happens along."

A look of terror came into poor Collins' face. He surrendered and fell to, and the way the eatables and drinkables disappeared was a sight for epicures. Half an hour later I peeped into the little saloon and there sat the young gentleman, his head on his arms, fast asleep in the midst of the wreck of his breakfast. The good-hearted steward explained that he had dropped off quite suddenly, and that he hated to disturb him, as he seemed to need rest so badly.

When the time came to spread the cloth for the mid-day meal he was gently awakened. Apologizing for having turned the saloon into a bedroom, he went on deck. Here he found Eaton and me awaiting, with appetites like those of young wolves, the first tinkle of the dinner bell.

We reached Yale before dark. I am sorry to say that I forgot all about Collins. Eaton went to an hotel, and I went to my own quarters back of the express office. My assistant at that time was Arthur Vann. He was expecting to hear any day of the death of his mother and said that when she died he would inherit a moderate fortune.

The next morning, while writing at my desk, I heard a foot-step. On looking up I saw my fellow passenger of the day before. He looked wan and ill, and black half circles under his eyes gave evidence of great weariness, if not of want of sleep.

"Are there any letters for Harry Collins?" he asked, timidly.

"None," replied Vann.

"Any for George Collins?"

The same answer was returned, and he was walking slowly away when I arose and asked him where he was staying in town?

"Nowhere," he replied.

"Nowhere!" I exclaimed. "Where did you stay last night?"

"I didn't stay anywhere. I just walked back and forth between here and the Indian village."

"Good gracious, man," I cried, "why did you not knock me up? I'd have given you a place to sleep. Have you had anything to eat today?"

"No, sir," he replied faintly. "And yesterday I had nothing but breakfast."

"Good God!" cried old Vann, as he seized him by the hand and fairly dragged him into the back room. The young fellow protested feebly; but it was of no use. Vann pushed him into a seat at the table and we soon had the satisfaction of seeing our guest eating heartily. Between mouthfuls he would murmur his thanks, while tears stole silently down his cheeks. As he ate, I recalled my own plight at San Francisco three years before where I walked the streets hungry and friendless for many hours until I met a classmate who loaned me sufficient to buy a meal. I felt thankful that I was enabled in a sense to repay that act of kindness by befriending this stranger.

The repast finished, Vann announced that he had fixed up a bed for the young fellow on a bale of blankets in the store, behind a screen of empty boxes, where he might sleep soundly till next day. Presently the grateful man stole off to bed, lying down with his clothes on. He slept all day, only awakening when Vann served him with a cup of tea and some buttered toast. When I looked out before retiring our guest was again wrapped in a heavy slumber.

In the morning he was still in bed and asleep, but while Vann was busily engaged in preparing our breakfast he rose and tried to steal off unobserved. Vann, however, was on the lookout for him, and made him wait for breakfast. After the meal, Collins insisted on helping to wash the dishes — a task that I always abhorred — and he proved himself well versed in the art of keeping a kitchen and its utensils clean. Vann soon began calling him Harry and making harmless jests which he enjoyed keenly.

There was resident in Yale at that time a woman who was known as Johanna Maguire. She was a turbulent, noisy, spiteful character, and when intoxicated, as she often was, she was looked upon as dangerous. She was said to be well connected in Ireland, and was accustomed to call at the express office for her letters each week on the arrival of a letter bag from below. On this particular morning the Maguire woman entered the office just as young Collins was passing out.

"Who's that?" asked the woman, sharply.

"Oh, a friend of the boss," explained Vann.

"Who is he?" she asked me.

"A friend of mine," I replied in an indifferent tone.

"A friend, is it?" she said, mockingly. "Fot's his name?"

"Oh, never mind," said I, testily "He's a good fellow, and that's enough for you to know."

"Good, is he? Good for what? Good for nothin'. Look out for him. I stared him square in the eye, and divil a bit would he look at me! There's somethin' wrong with him, I tell ye."

I saw that the woman was in one of her worst moods. I knew that unless I conquered her then she would never again treat me with respect. So I prepared for a tussle.

"Johanna," I said, "listen to me. You never come here that you have not something to say that you ought not to say about someone. Sometimes I come under the harrow of your tongue. At others it is a woman whose only misfortune is that she has to breathe the same air you do. And now it's this friendless boy. You must stop the flow of your evil tongue or cease coming here at all."

The woman turned red and then white with rage. "Hould your own tongue or it'll be the wuss for ye. Things has come to a pretty pass when a brat the likes of you dares talk to a woman that's ould enough to be — to be —"

"His mother?" I cut in. I could not help it; the temptation was great.

I thought she would have brained me with a heavy weight that lay on the counter. She made a spring forward, but restrained herself with difficulty, and with white, quivering lips demanded to be told what I would do to her if she did not behave herself.

"Would I trow her into the strate?"

"No," I said, "but I'll write to Mr. Ballou and tell him to send no more of your letters by express. They will then come on a week later by mail, if they get here at all. You are not fit to come in contact with the decent men and women who come here."

To my surprise she turned her face towards the door and walked slowly out. Ten minutes later she came back, and extending her hand, said: "I want yez to fergive me; I'll be good as gowld after this. Sure, I meant no ha-r-r-m to the bye or to ye, but I have the divil's own timper, and that added to a dhrop of rum I took down the strate just upset me intirely." So we shook hands. The woman never afterwards misbehaved herself while in my establishment, and I was not a little proud of my victory.

The next day I got work for Collins on a claim that I was interested in on Yale Bar. He continued to sleep in the outer office, and every morning he would light the fire and get everything in readiness for Vann's cooking, besides helping to "rid up," as he called it. In the evening, after helping to "rid up," he retired to his rude couch.

He neither smoked nor played cards. He did not drink or swear. Vann, who did all four with the usual trimmings, suddenly dropped them. When anything went wrong — for instance, when a cup or saucer fell on the floor and was smashed — instead of sending an oath after it, he took to whistling a favorite tune. One day Vann told me that on rising rather earlier than usual he had found Harry on his knees beside the bale of blankets, evidently praying.

"Now," said the old man, "he didn't know that I seen him, so I just sneaked away in my stocking feet. I go my pile on a man who prays by himself, and don't let anyone but God see or hear him."

Harry was never out of temper, and was always willing to do his share of the house work. But he had a sad, pensive way about him which quite baffled all my efforts to penetrate. Vann sized him up as in love. I resolved that when that big brother of his came down the trail I would ask him what was the matter with the boy.

One day, about a week after we had taken the young man in, Vann came to me with an open letter in his hand.

"My mother's dead," he said. "She's gone and I'm rich. I resign my position at once, for I must go down the river tomorrow. I'll tell you what to do. Put young Collins into my place. He's just the man for you."

I went at once down to the claim. There I saw Collins standing on top of a long range of sluice boxes, armed with a sluice fork, engaged in clearing the riffles of large stones and sticks which would obstruct the passage of water and gravel and prevent the capture of the tiny specks of gold by the quicksilver with which the riffles were charged.

On the way I met the foreman. He was in a white rage because I had sent a "counter-jumper," a mere whipper-snapper, to do a miner's work. He had tried him at the shovel and pick, and he was too weak to handle them, and so he had put him at the lightest job on the sluices. "He won't take off his coat like the other boys, and all the men are threatening to strike because they have to do harder work for the same pay that he's getting. There he stands, with his long duster flapping in the wind, like a pillow-case on a clothesline," concluded the foreman with a look of disgust on his face.

"Never mind, Bill," said I. "You won't be troubled with him any more. I have a better job for him."

"I pity the job," said Bill.

I passed down to where Collins was at work and told him of Vann's fortune and his own promotion. He accompanied me back to the office where he was duly installed. Collins proved to be an excellent cook, as neat as any housewife, and a fairly good bookkeeper. But I could never induce him to sleep in the bed that had been vacated by Vann until he had removed it into the outer office. He said the back room was too small for two people, and that the air was better in the larger room.

Of every miner who came into the office from above the canyon, Collins made anxious inquiries about his brother. Did they know him by name, or had they met anyone who answered to the description which he gave them? The answers were always negative, but he never despaired and every failure seemed only to incite him to renewed inquiries.

The months of July and August 1859 were unusually dry and the weather was sultry. Every evening, after Collins had "rid up" the kitchen, he would sit on a box in front of the store and listen to the wonderful tales of gold finds as they were narrated by miners and prospectors. He would never utter a word, but would listen, with his big blue eyes wide open, as if the tales astonished and entranced him.

One night, I remember, the full moon shone brightly upon the group that had gathered near the door, and the rays seemed to rest like a halo of silver about the boy's head and face. His profile was delicate and expressive, and as I gazed I felt strongly and unaccountably drawn towards him. A strange emotion stirred my heart and a wave of tenderness such as I had never before experienced swept through every fibre of my being. What ails me, I asked myself?

As if in answer to my mental question, the boy turned his head and looked in my direction. When he saw that I was observing him he dropped his eyes and, rising quickly, gazed long and anxiously in the direction of the canyon and at the sullen river which roared loudly on its way to the ocean. Then he sighed deeply, breathed a gentle "goodnight," and retired to his bed in the corner.

"The boy turned his head and looked in my direction."

Below: Yale's main street which in the early 1860s fronted the Fraser River.

Long after the company had departed I sat and mused. I could not understand my feelings. Why should I be attracted towards him more than to any other young man? Why was I always happy when he was near and depressed when he was absent? Why did I lie awake at night trying to work out some plan to send word to his brother? Why did the sound of his voice or his footstep send the hot young blood bounding through my veins? What was he to me that every sense should thrill, and my heart beat wildly at his approach? Were the mysterious forces of Nature making themselves heard and felt?

I am not sure as to the precise date or the month when the circumstance I am about to relate took place. It was, however, either in the latter part of August or the early part of September 1859, nearly four months after I had first met Collins on the steamer. He came to me one afternoon and complained of feeling very sick, almost as if he would die. I told him to go into my room and lie down in my bunk, which he did.

In the bustle and hurry of receiving and dispatching a letter and treasure express I forgot all about the boy and his troubles. Two or three hours later, when recalling his illness, I asked the Maguire woman, who had entered the office for a letter and who had lately taken to patronizing the boy, to see how he was getting on. She was inside for about five minutes. Then, coming out on tiptoe as softly as a cat in pursuit of a mouse, she asked me, in a whisper, to go at once for Dr. Fifer, the leading surgeon at the time. "The bye's very sick. He's all of a shiver. I think he's got the cholery morbus."

I summoned Fifer, and was about to enter the room when Johanna barred my entrance, and requested me for "the good Lord's sake to shtay out. The bye must be kept quiet."

I rebelled at this treatment, and was preparing for another verbal conflict when the doctor came to her assistance and added his entreaty to hers. So I remained out, but determined to have an explanation later on. As I was fuming and fretting over the impropriety of keeping a man from entering his own room the doctor came out with a puzzled look on his face.

"Really," he commenced, "this is a most remarkable case. It beats everything. In all my experience I never saw anything like it. How long have you known Collins?"

I told him about four months.

"Humph! Really this is extraordinary — most extraordinary."

What he would have said further will never be recorded, for at that moment the shrill voice of Johanna Maguire was heard.

"Docther, come quick! come quick!"

The doctor rushed inside, and in five or six minutes came out again. He put his hand on my shoulder and looking me full in the face said, "It's my duty to tell you that Harry Collins is no more!"

"Mercy!" I cried, shrinking back, "Not dead? not dead?"

"Well, no, not dead; but you'll never see him again."

"If he is not dead," I said, greatly agitated, "tell me what has happened or why I shall never see him again. You should not keep me in suspense."

"Well," said the doctor, laughing heartily, "he is not dead. He's very much alive. That is to say, he is doubly alive. Harry Collins is gone, but in his place there is a comely young woman who calls herself Harriet Collins, the wife of George Collins, who is now above the canyon hunting for gold. She has just been delivered of a handsome girl baby that weighs at least seven pounds.

"That is all there is about it except that if any of your lady friends have any women's dresses or babies' clothes that they want to give away, the late Harry Collins — and present Mrs. George Collins — will be mighty glad to get them. With the exception of your blankets and your underwear, which Mrs. Maguire has appropriated for the purpose, she has nothing to wrap the baby in."

"Didn't I tell you," said Johanna the next day, "to watch that bye. I knowed there was something wrong about him, and I was roight. But I have looked out for yer charakther and mine, too. Before I'd do a hand's turn I made her show me the marriage lines, and here they are. She wants you to see them."

The "lines" were a certificate of the marriage by the Reverend Dr. Scott, of San Francisco, of George Collins and Harriet Hurst, less than a year before.

The ladies of Yale very liberally gave Mrs. Collins dresses and undergarments from their own wardrobes for herself and her baby. There was only one sewing machine in the town, and it was soon at work, altering and making garments for the mother and the little stranger. On the third day I was admitted to the presence of the young mother and her first-born. She asked my forgiveness for the deception she had practised. She said that it was a desire to be near her husband, and also the cruel treatment of a stepmother, that had induced her to seek him without money or friends and in male attire.

Tommy Eaton and I set our wits to work to find the husband. We were unsuccessful until one day, some four weeks after the arrival of the little girl, a tall, travel-stained young man entered the express office and asked if there was a letter for George Collins.

Eaton told him there was none for him.

"Are there any packages — I expect a valuable one from San Francisco?" he said.

"No, there are no packages of any kind for George Collins," was the reply. "But here's the agent, ask him," as I stepped into the office.

"Any package for George Collins"

"Is that your name?"

"Yes," he said.

"Well, if you are the right George Collins, there are two most valuable packages awaiting you here, but you will have to be identified before you can get them," I said.

"I know no one in Yale," he replied.

"Then," said I, "come with me into the back room and see if they belong to you?"

As we walked towards the room the door was flung back. An apparition, clad in white with outstretched hands and eyes wide open and staring, stood suddenly framed in the opening.

"George! George!" the apparition wildly cried. "Oh! I knew your voice. I would know it among a million. My dear, dear husband, God has answered my prayers and brought you back to me safe and sound. I am so tired, so tired." She tottered and would have fallen had not the young man sprung forward and folded her in his great arms.

As they retired within the room I closed the door and was turning away when I heard a noise as of someone sobbing. I turned. There stood Tommy Eaton with his handkerchief to his eyes, crying as if his heart would break.

"You big chump," I began. "You ought to be ashamed of yourself. What business—?" I never finished the sentence. I couldn't; and it has not been finished to this day.

The great news spread rapidly. The town, which had begun to recover from the excitement consequent upon the arrival of the baby, was again thrown into a state of extreme agitation by the arrival of the father and husband. Collins proved to be a young man of some means, but Mrs. Maguire declined any remuneration. In about a month it was announced that the pair would leave for California.

First they went around and said goodbye to those who had befriended them. When they knocked at Johanna Maguire's door she came outside. "Sure," said she, "I'll not ask ye in; but I give ye me blessing, and a piece of gowld for the baby." She pressed a nugget into the proud mother's hand, and continued, "I want to ask one favor of ye. Let me kiss the baby's hand — sure I'm not good enough to kiss its lips."

She raised the hand to her mouth and covered it with kisses. Then she lifted the hem of the mother's garment to her lips and was about to kiss it, when Mrs. Collins, tearing the garment from her grasp, threw her arms about the poor, lost one. She kissed her not once but a dozen times, saying that she was her own kindest and best friend, who had gone with her through the dark valley and shadow of death and wooed her back to life with motherly care and attention, and invoking Heaven's choicest blessing on her head. In the midst of a torrent of tears the woman tore herself away and, rushing into her house, slammed the door violently and was not seen again for several days.

Some weeks after Mr. and Mrs. Collins had gone away, engraved cards for the christening at San Francisco of a mite to be named Caledonia H. Collins were received by nearly everyone in Yale. Mine was accompanied by an explanatory note that the "H" stood for my surname, and that I was to be the godfather. Johanna's invitation was accompanied by a pretty gold watch and a loving letter from her late patient.

Nine years sped away before I was enabled to visit San Francisco, but diligent enquiries failed to discover any trace of the Collins family. They had moved and I have never since heard of or from them. Somewhere on the face of this globe there should be a mature female who rejoices in the name of Caledonia H. Collins. I would be glad to learn her whereabouts, for I would travel many miles to meet the woman who under such extraordinary circumstances became my god-daughter.

The Farewell Banquet

It was to be a memorable occasion for the departing businessman and it was — but for reasons unexpected and tragic

---

On a pleasant evening early in April 1861, Victoria's Hotel de France was a scene of interest, brilliancy and activity. John Kurtz, a leading citizen of Yale, a man who had been foremost in works and ventures of public utility, was on his way out of the country with the object of taking up his residence in California. Fortune had favored the man in all his doings. On leaving Yale he had been presented with an expensive gold watch, duly inscribed, and a heavy gold chain, as an expression of the goodwill of his fellow citizens. At Victoria he was tendered a banquet by thirty or forty friends who had watched his career and who, to a certain extent, had prospered through his undertakings.

One of this good citizen's achievements had been to solve the problem of steamboat navigation to Yale. None of the steamers of the regular transportation lines would venture above Fort Hope, sixteen miles below, where freight was discharged into canoes and barges and towed by manual labor to Yale. John Kurtz had contended that a steamboat might be built that would make the passage from Victoria to Yale with ease and in perfect safety. He recalled that in 1858 the sternwheel steamer *Umatilla* had made the passage on two occasions during high water, and he argued that what had been done once could be done again. So he formed the Yale Steam Navigation Company, with a capital of $40,000. The money was quickly raised and the new steamer was built at Laing's ways in Victoria.

On her first trip she skimmed the troubled waters like a huge bird. Skilfully handled, she avoided rocks, bars and riffles and landed her cargo at Yale on the second day. Returning, she left Yale in the morning, and the same evening landed passengers and freight at Victoria. All promised well for the new company and their new boat. Stock was at a premium. On all hands they were congratulated, and at the time the banquet was laid the *Fort Yale* was preparing for another trip, and filling up rapidly with freight and already had all her passenger space taken.

The night selected for the banquet was the close of a charming day, as I have said. The table was laid in the restaurant of the hotel and every viand and liquid that would stimulate and coax the appetite were there in abundance.

Among the guests were Thomas Harris, the first mayor of Victoria; George Pearkes, Solicitor-General; Captain Jamieson, of the steamboat *Fort Yale*; Honorable Dr. Helmcken, Speaker of the first Legislative Assembly ever convened on the British Pacific; the gifted Amor De Cosmos, afterwards Premier; and a score of others whose names escape me at this writing.

The dinner was served in the style for which the Hotel de France was then famous, and when the toasts had been drunk, the fun waxed fast and furious. Midnight struck from the hotel clock, but no one stirred.

It had been arranged that the whole party — or at least those who could find their legs — should proceed to Esquimalt, then the place of departure of the California steamers, and there bid the parting guest Godspeed. The steamer was announced to sail at six the following morning. As the night wore on the older members retired, but the wild revel continued, and when everyone was in a merry mood a card was handed to Mr. Kurtz by one of the waiters. The recipient excused himself for a moment and presently returned and, addressing the chairman, said:

"An English gentleman whom I met a few days ago at Yale is outside, and desires to join the party if agreeable to all. His name is Esdale, and he is a nephew of Lord Portman."

"Bring him in, by all means," cried one and all, and a young fellow of about five-and-twenty entered. The newcomer was of medium size; dark, almost swarthy. He was neatly dressed, and had the appearance and bearing of an English gentleman. He was conducted to a vacant chair at the side of the guest of the evening — said chair having been vacated by one of the company who had found the conviviality too vigorous for his comfort.

In a few minutes Lord Portman's nephew was on the best of terms with the whole company. Such a beaming, sunny face, lighted up by a pair of bright, black eyes and a radiating smile that seemed to be "catching," as one of the company remarked, for it put us all in a good humor and kept us there.

Jim McCrea, who was a famous raconteur, had just told one of his characteristic stories, and the chairman had sung an Italian ditty in a sweet tenor, when the health of Mr. Kurtz was proposed. Mr. Kurtz responded and sat down, when Mr. Esdale asked permission to say a few words. The request was granted, whereupon he delivered one of the most eloquent and witty after-dinner speeches that it has ever been my good fortune to hear. He spoke for only about ten minutes, but when he concluded the company rose and drank the health of "Lord Portman's nephew" with a "hip! hip! hurrah!" and "He's a jolly good fellow." He responded with another witty address.

The most popular man at that table, with the exception of "our guest," was Mr. Esdale. Everyone begged the favor of a glass of wine with him. He had evidently dined generously before he came to us, but his holding capacity seemed unlimited. He drank with every one who offered, and was none the worse for it, so far as we could see.

About two o'clock a practice then much in vogue at "stag" dinner parties was introduced. Every guest was required to sing a song, tell a story or dance a jig, and when Esdale's turn came he did all three, gracefully and well. McCrea, who was noted as the town wit, was completely outdone by this new competitor for convivial honors and declared that from thenceforth he would not crack a joke nor tell a story.

Daylight was creeping in at the window when the rigs that were to carry us to Esquimalt drove up at the hotel door. Of course the drivers must have something. So they were had in to partake of the food and wine, and as a consequence more than one of their number presently gave outward and visible signs of too much good cheer. Esdale, who was in prime condition, acted as host, many of the others having become incapacitated. I was seated near the head of the table, and Esdale was handing a glass of wine to a driver when his foot seemed to slip and he fell forward on the table. Quickly recovering himself, he smiled at his awkwardness and, declining assistance, sat down.

I watched him narrowly and saw an ashen hue steal slowly over his face. His eyes rolled and then became fixed and stared at one of the coal-oil lamps. The next instant he fell heavily forward. In a moment the scene of mirth and revelry was changed to one of dismay and confusion. Some went to the aid of the stricken man, others flew for a doctor. Dr. Helmcken and Dr. Trimble had gone home. Unfortunately, there was a doctor in the house at the time. His name was Ramsey, a young and inexperienced graduate. He was hastily summoned. In his ignorance he pronounced the trouble *delirium tremens* and prescribed a composing draught — the very thing he should not have done for the young man was suffering from a stroke of apoplexy. Presently the inevitable occurred. Death entered as the Unbidden Guest and bore away the bright, witty, handsome and culti-

Among survivors of the *Fort Yale* explosion were Captain John Irving, top left, and Francis J. Barnard. Irving became a popular Fraser River steamboatman and when he died in 1872 flags in New Westminster were flown at half mast. Barnard became equally well known. He founded the B.C. Express Company, whose red and yellow stagecoaches served the Cariboo for over 50 years.

vated Esdale, Lord Portman's nephew.

The presence of death had a sobering influence on all who attended the party. The arranged excursion to Esquimalt was not carried out. Mr. Kurtz went almost unattended to the steamer, and the guests, saddened and sobered by the awful event, wended their ways sorrowfully homeward. But another tradedy was about to unfold.

Captain Jamieson had left the festive board early in the evening and his fine steamboat sailed for Yale. At Fort Hope, Captain William Irving and Frank J. Barnard of this city joined the vessel. As the steamer approached the first bad riffle above Hope, Captain Irving was with Captain Jamieson in the pilot-house. Just then dinner was announced, and Captain Irving offered to take the wheel while Captain Jamieson went to the table. The offer was declined.

Captain Irving had scarcely taken his seat when, with a loud roar, the boiler exploded. In an instant the pride of the river became a helpless hulk, drifting down stream. A dozen people were killed or injured. Among the former was Captain Jamieson whose body was never recovered. Had Captain Irving's offer been accepted he would have been the victim instead of his friend.

The cause of the explosion was never known. The Yale Steam Navigation Company went out of business and many years elapsed before another boat ventured to make the hazardous trip.

A Russian princess, a California quartz mine
and a pretty young girl with some poetry
were an unexpected part of

My First Christmas Dinner
in Victoria, 1860

On December 22, 1860, I sat in the editorial room of the *Colonist* office on Wharf Street preparing a leading article. Mr. De Cosmos, the editor and owner, had contracted a severe cold and was confined to his room so the entire work of writing up the paper for that issue devolved upon me. Our office was a rude affair. The editorial room was a small space partitioned off from the composing-room, which contained also the little hand-press on which the paper was printed. A person who might wish to see the editor was forced to pick his way through a line of stands and cases, at which stood the coatless printers who set the type and prepared the forms for the press.

The day was chill and raw. A heavy wind from the southwest stirred the waters of the harbour and, hurling itself with fury against the front of the building, made the timbers crack and groan as if in paroxysms of pain. A driving rain fell in sheets on the roof, and drops of water which leaked through the shingles fell on the editorial table, swelled into little rivulets and, leaping to the floor, chased each other across the room, making existence therein uncomfortably damp.

As I wrote away in spite of these obstacles, I was made aware by a shadow that fell across my table of the presence of someone in the doorway. I raised my eyes and there stood a female — a rare object when women and children were as scarce as hen's teeth and were hardly ever met upon the streets, much less in an editorial sanctum. I rose to my feet. In the brief space that elapsed before the lady spoke, I took her all in. She was a woman of scarcely forty, I thought; of medium height, a brunette, with

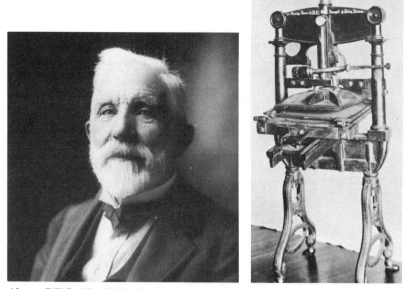

Above: Bill Smith left Halifax for California where he changed his name to Amor de Cosmos. He followed the gold rush north to Victoria and used this printing press to issue his first *British Colonist* on December 11, 1858. The Wharf Street office below is where Higgins joined him a short time later as a reporter.

Photo. by R. Maynard

large coal-black eyes, a pretty mouth — a perfect Cupid's bow — and olive-hued cheeks. She was richly dressed in bright colors, with heavy broad stripes and space-encircling hoops after the fashion of the day. When she spoke it was in a rich, well-rounded tone. Taken all in all, I sized the lady up as a very presentable person. When I explained to her in response to an enquiry that the editor was ill, she said that she would call again, and went away after leaving her card.

Two days later the lady came again. "Is the editor still ill?" she asked.

"Yes; but he will be here in the course of a day or two."

"Ah! Well, that is too bad," she said. "My business is of importance and cannot bear delay. But I am told that you will do as well."

I assured the lady that I should be glad to assist her in any way. Thanking me, she began:

"My name is Madame Fabre. My husband died in California. I am a Russian. In Russia I am a princess." (She paused as if to watch the impression her announcement had made.) "Here I am a mere nobody — only Madame Fabre. I married my husband in France. We came to California. We had much money and my husband went into quartz mining at Grass Valley. He did not understand the business at all. We lost everything. Then he died. He left me a mountain of debts and one son, Bertrand, a good child, as good as gold, very thoughtful and obedient. May I call him in? He awaits your permission without."

I replied, "Certainly." Stepping to the door, she called, "Bertrand! Bertrand! my child, come here, and speak to the gentleman."

I expected to see a curly haired boy of five or six years, in short pants, a beaded jacket and fancy cap, whom I would take on my knee, toy with his curls and ask his name and age. Judge of my surprise when, preceded by the noise of a heavy tread, a huge youth of about seventeen, bigger and taller than myself, and smoking a cigar, appeared at the opening. In a deep, gruff voice that a sea captain or a militia commander would have envied, he asked, "Did you call, mamma?"

"Yes, my dear child," she sweetly responded, "I wish to introduce you to this gentleman."

The "child" removed his hat, and I noticed that his hair was cut close to the scalp. Having been duly introduced, at my request he sat down in my chair. The mother gazed at her son fondly for a moment and then proceeded:

"Bertrand's fortune was swallowed up in the quartz wreck, but he is very sweet and very patient, and never complains. Poor lad, it was hard upon him, but he forgives all — do you not, dear?"

"Yes," rumbled the "child" from the pit of his stomach. But the expression that flitted across his visage made me think that he would rather have said "No" had he dared.

"That being the case I will now explain the object of my visit. As I have said, we have lost everything — that is to say, our income is so greatly reduced that it is now a matter of not more than $1,000 a month. Upon that meagre sum my dear boy and I contrive to get along by practising the strictest economy consistent with our position in life. Naturally we wish to do better and then go back to Russia and live with the nobility. Do we not, Bertrand?"

"Yes," rumbled the "child" from his stomach again, as he lighted a fresh cigar.

"Well, now," the lady went on, "I want an adviser. I ask Pierre Manciot at the French Hotel and he tells me to see his partner, John Sere; and Mr. Sere tells me to go to the editor of the *Colonist*. I come here."

She paused for a moment to take a newspaper from her reticule and then continued:

"After my husband died and left the debts and this precious child" (the "child" gazed abstractedly at the ceiling while he blew rings of smoke from his mouth) "we make a grand discovery. Our foreman, working in the mine, strikes rich quartz, covers it up again, and tells no one but me. All the shareholders have gone — what you called 'busted,' I believe? We get hold of many shares cheap, and now I come here to get the rest. An Englishman owns enough shares to give him control — I mean that out of 200,000 shares I have got 95,000 and the rest this Englishman holds. We have traced him through Oregon to this place, and we lose all sign of him here." (Up to this moment I had not been particularly interested in the narration.) She paused, and laying a neatly-gloved hand on my arm proceeded:

"You are a man of affairs."

I modestly intimated that I was nothing of the kind, only a reporter.

"Ah! yes. You cannot deceive me. I see it in your eye, your face, your movements. You are a man of large experience and keen judgment. Your conversation is charming."

As she had spoken for ten minutes without giving me an opportunity to say a word, I could not quite understand how she arrived at an estimate of my conversational powers. However, I felt flattered, but said nothing.

Pressing my arm with her hand, she went on:

"I come to you as a man of the world. (I made a gesture of dissent, but it was very feeble, for I was already caught in the web.) "I rely upon you. I ask you to help me."

Was it possible that because I was considered unredeemably bad I was selected for this woman's purpose? As I mused, half disposed to get angry, I raised my head and my eyes encountered the burning orbs of Madame, gazing full into mine. They seemed to bore like gimlets into my very soul. A thrill ran through me like the shock from an electric battery, and in an instant I seemed bound hand and foot to the fortunes of this strange woman. I felt myself being dragged along as the Roman Emperors were wont to draw their captives through the streets of their capital. I have only a hazy recollection of what passed between us after that, but I call to mind that she asked me to insert as an advertisement a paragraph from a Grass Valley newspaper to the effect that the mine (the name of which I forget) was a failure and that shares could be bought for two cents.

When she took her leave I promised to call upon her at the hotel. When the "child" extended a cold, clammy hand in farewell I felt like giving him a kick — he looked so grim and ugly and patronizing. I gazed into his eyes sternly and read there deceit, hypocrisy and moral degeneration. How I hated him!

The pair had been gone several minutes before I recovered my mental balance and awoke to a realization that I was a young fool who had sold himself (perhaps to the devil) for a few empty compliments and a peep into the deep well of an artful woman's blazing eyes.

I was inwardly cursing my stupidity, while pacing up and down the floor, when I heard a timid knock at the door. In response to my invitation to "come in" a young lady entered. She was pretty and about twenty, fair, with dark eyes and light brown hair. A blush suffused her face as she asked for the editor. I returned the usual answer.

"Perhaps you will do for my purpose," she said, timidly. "I have here a piece of poetry."

I gasped as I thought, "It's an ode on winter. Oh, Caesar!"

"A piece of poetry," she continued, "on 'Britain's Queen.' If you will read it and find it worthy a place in your paper I shall be glad to write more. If it is worth paying for I shall be glad to get anything."

Her hand trembled as she produced the paper.

I thanked her, telling her that I would look it over and she withdrew. I could not help contrasting the first with the last visitor. The one had attracted me by her artful and flattering tongue, the skillful use of her beautiful eyes and the pressure of her hand on my coat sleeve; the other, by the modesty of her demeanor.

The timid shyness with which she presented her poem had caught my fancy. I looked at the piece. It was poor; not but what the sentiment was there — the ideas were good, but they were not well put. As prose it would have been acceptable, but as verse it was impossible and not worth anything.

The next day was Christmas Day. It was my first Christmas in Victoria. Business was suspended. All the stores were closed. At that time in front of every business house there was a wooden verandah or shed that extended from the front of the building to the outer edge of the sidewalk. One might walk along any of the down-town streets and be under cover all the way. They were ugly, unsightly constructions, and I waged constant warfare against them until I joined the aldermanic board and secured the passage of an ordinance that compelled their removal.

Along these verandahs on this particular Christmas morning evergreen boughs were placed, and the little town really presented a very pretty and sylvan appearance. After church I went to the office and from the office to the Hotel de France for luncheon. The only other guest in the room was a tall, florid-faced young man somewhat older than myself. He occupied a table on the opposite side of the room. When I gave my order one of the owners, M. Sere, remarked, "All the regular boarders but you have gone to luncheon and dinner with their friends. Why not you?"

"Why," I replied, with a quaver in my voice, "the only families that I know are dining with friends of their own whom I do not know. I feel more homesick today than ever before in my life and the idea of eating my Christmas dinner alone fills me with melancholy thoughts."

The man on the other side of the room must have overheard me for he said, "There's two of a kind. I'm in a similar fix. I have no friends here — at least none with whom I can dine. Suppose we double up?"

"What's that?" I asked.

"Why, let us eat our Christmas dinner together and have a good time. Here's my card and here's a letter of credit on Mr. Pendergast — Wells, Fargo's agent — to show that I am not without visible means of support."

The card read, "Mr. George Barclay, Grass Valley."

"Why," I said, "you are from Grass Valley. How strange! I saw two people yesterday, a lady and her 'child,' who claimed to have come from Grass Valley."

"Indeed," he asked, "what are they like?"

"The mother says she is a Russian princess. She calls herself Mme. Fabre and says she is a widow. She is very handsome and intelligent, and," I added with a shudder, "has the loveliest eyes — they bored me through and through."

My new-found friend faintly smiled and said, "I know them.

By-and-bye, when we get better acquainted, I shall tell you all about them. Meantime, be on your guard."

After luncheon we walked back to the *Colonist* shack. As I placed the key in the lock I saw the young lady who had submitted the poetry walking rapidly towards us. My companion flushed slightly and extended his hand, which the lady accepted with hesitation. Then the lady, addressing me, asked, "Was my poem acceptable?"

"To tell you the truth, Miss — Miss —"

"Forbes," she interjected.

"I have not had time to read it carefully." (As a matter of fact I had not bestowed a second thought upon the poem, but was ashamed to acknowledge it.)

"When — oh! when can you decide?" she asked with much earnestness.

"Tomorrow, I think —?" I fully intended to decline it.

She seemed deeply disappointed. Her lip quivered as she held down her head, and her form trembled with agitation. I could not understand her emotion, but, of course, said nothing to show that I observed it.

"Could you not give me an answer today — this afternoon," the girl eagerly urged.

"Yes," I said, "as you seem so very anxious, if you will give me your address I shall take or send an answer before four o'clock. Where do you reside?"

"Do you know Forshay's cottages? We occupy No. 4."

Forshay's cottages were a collection of little cabins, each containing three rooms — a kitchen and two other rooms. I could scarcely imagine a refined person such as the lady before me occupying those miserable quarters, but then necessity knows no law.

The girl thanked me, and Barclay accompanied her to the corner of Yates Street. He seemed to be trying to induce her to do something she did not approve of, for she shook her head with an air of determination and hurried away.

Barclay came back to the office and said: "I am English myself, but the silliest creature in the world is an Englishman who, having once been well off, finds himself stranded. His pride will not allow him to accept favors. I knew that girl's father and mother in Grass Valley. The old gentleman lost a fortune at quartz mining. His partner, a Mr. Maloney, having sunk his own and his wife's money in the mine, poisoned his wife, three children and himself with strychnine three years ago. By the way, I met a Grass Valley man this morning. His name is Robert Homfray, a civil engineer. He tells me he is located here permanently.

"He and his brother lost a great deal of money in the Grass Valley mines, and we talked over the Maloney tragedy, with the circumstances of which he was familiar. The strangest part of the story is that three months ago the property was reopened and the first shot that was fired in the tunnel laid bare a rich vein. Had Maloney fired one more charge he would have been rich. As it was he died a murderer and a suicide. Poor fellow! In a day or two I will tell you more. But let us return to the poetry. What will you do with it?"

"I fear I shall have to reject it."

"No! no!" he cried. "Accept it! This morning I went to the home of the family, which consists of Mr. Forbes, who is crippled with rheumatism, his excellent wife, the young lady from whom we have just parted, and a little boy of seven. They are in actual want. I offered to lend them money to buy common necessaries, and Forbes rejected the offer in language that was insulting. Go immediately to the cottage. Tell the girl that you have accepted the poem and give her this (handing me a $20 gold piece) as the appraised value of her production. Then return to the Hotel de France and await developments."

I repaired to the cottages. The road was long and muddy. There was neither sidewalks nor streets, and it was a difficult matter to navigate the sea of mud. The young lady answered my knock. She almost fainted when I told her the poem had been accepted and that the fee was $20. I placed the coin in her hand.

"Mamma! Papa!" she cried and, running inside the house, I heard her say, "My poem has been accepted, and the gentleman from the *Colonist* office has brought me $20."

"Thank God!" I heard a woman's voice exclaim. "I never lost faith."

This was followed by a sound as of some one crying, and then the girl flew back to the door. "Oh, sir," she said, "I thank you from the bottom of my heart for your goodness."

"Not at all," I said. "You have earned it, and you owe me no thanks. I shall be glad to receive and pay for any other contributions you may send." I did not add, though, that they would not be published, although they would be paid for.

A little boy with a troubled face and a pinched look now approached the front door. He was neatly but poorly dressed.

"Oh! Nellie, what is the matter?" he said, anxiously.

"Johnnie," answered Nellie, "I have earned $20, and we shall have a Christmas dinner, and you shall have a drum, too." As she said this she caught the little fellow in her arms and kissed him, and pressed his wan cheek against her own.

"Shall we have a turkey, Nellie?" he asked.

"Yes, dear," she said.

"And a plum pudding, too, with nice sauce that burns when you put a match to it, and shall I have two helpings?" he asked.

"Yes, and you shall set fire to the sauce, and have two helpings, Johnnie."

"Won't that be nice," he exclaimed, gleefully. "But, Nellie, will papa get medicine to make him well again?"

"Yes, Johnnie."

"And mamma — will she get back all the pretty things she sent away to pay the rent with?"

"Hush, Johnnie," said the girl, with an apologetic look at me.

"And you, Nellie, will you get back your warm cloak that the man with the long nose took away?"

"Hush, dear," she said. "Go inside now; I wish to speak to this gentleman." She closed the front door and asked me, all the stores being closed, how she would be able to get the materials for the dinner and to redeem her promise to Johnnie.

"Easily enough," said I. "Order it at the Hotel de France. Shall I take down the order?"

"If you will be so kind," she said. "Please order what you think is necessary."

"And I — I have a favor to ask of you."

"What is it?" she eagerly inquired.

"That you will permit me to eat my Christmas dinner with you and the family. I am a waif and stray, alone in the world. I am almost a stranger here. The few acquaintances I have made are dining out, and I am at the hotel with Mr. Barclay, whom you know, and I hope, esteem."

"Well," she said, "come, by all means."

"And may I bring Mr. Barclay with me? He is very lonely and very miserable. Just think that on a day like this he has nowhere to go but to an hotel."

She considered a moment before replying; then she said, "No, do not bring him — let him come in while we are at dinner, as if by accident."

I hastened to the Hotel de France, and Sere soon had a big hamper packed with an abundance of Christmas cheer and on its way upon the back of an Indian to the Forbes house.

I followed and received a warm welcome from the father and mother, who were superior people and gave every evidence of having seen better days. The interior was scrupulously clean, but there was only one chair. A small kitchen stove, at which the sick man sat, was the only means of warmth. There were no carpets, and if I was not mistaken, the bed coverings were scant.

The evidence of extreme poverty was everywhere manifest. I never felt meaner in my life than as I accepted the blessings that belonged to the other man. Mr. Forbes, who was too ill to sit at the table, reclined on a rude lounge near the kitchen stove. Just as dinner was being served there came a knock at the door. It was opened and there stood Barclay.

"I have come," he said, "to ask you to take me in. I cannot eat my dinner alone at the hotel. You have taken my only acquaintance (pointing to me) from me, and if Mr. Forbes will forgive my indiscretion about money this morning I shall be thankful."

"That I will," cried the old gentleman, from the kitchen. "Come in and let us shake hands and forget our differences."

So Barclay entered, and we ate our Christmas dinner in one of the bedrooms. It was laid on the kitchen table, upon which a table cloth, sent by the thoughtful hosts at the hotel, was spread. There were napkins, a big turkey, and claret and champagne, and a real, live, polite little Frenchman to carve and wait.

For a catch-up meal it was the jolliest I ever sat down to, and I enjoyed it, as did all the rest. Little Johnnie got two helpings of turkey and two helpings of pudding.

Barclay and I reached our quarters at the Hotel de France about midnight. We were a pair of thoroughly happy mortals, for had we not, after all, "dined out," and had we not had a royal good time on Christmas Day, 1860?

The morrow was Boxing Day, and none of the offices were opened. I saw nothing of the Princess; but I observed Bertie, the sweet "child," as he paid frequent visits to the bar and filled himself to the throttle with brandy and water and rum and gin, and bought and paid for and smoked the best cigars at two bits each. As I gazed upon him the desire to give him a kicking grew stronger.

By appointment, Barclay and I met in a private room at the hotel where he unfolded his plans.

"You must have seen," he began, "that Miss Forbes and I are warm friends. Our friendship began six months ago. I proposed to her, and was accepted, subject to the approval of the father. He refused to give his consent because, having lost his money, he could not give his daughter a dowry. It was in vain I urged that I had sufficient for both. He would listen to nothing that involved an acceptance of assistance from me, and he left for Vancouver Island to try his fortunes there. He fell ill, and they have sold or pawned everything of value. The girl was not permitted to bid me goodbye when they left Grass Valley.

"After their departure the discovery of which I have informed you was made in the Maloney tunnel, and as Mr. Forbes has held on to a control of the stock in spite of his adversities, he is now a rich man. I want to marry the girl. As I told you, I proposed when I believed them to be ruined. It is now my duty to acquaint the family with their good fortune, and renew my suit. I think I ought to do it today.

I told him I thought he should impart the good news at once. He left me for that purpose. As I walked into the dining room, I saw the dear "child" Bertrand leaning over the bar quaffing a glass of absinthe. When he saw me he gulped down the drink and said "Mamma would like to speak to you — she thought you would have called."

I recalled the adventure with the eyes and hesitated. Then I decided to go to Room 12 on the second flat and see the thing out. A knock on the door was responded to by a sweet "Come in." Mme. Fabre was seated in an easy chair before a cheerful fire.

She rose at once and extended a plump and white hand. As we seated ourselves she flashed her burning eyes upon me and said:

"I am so glad you have come. I do want your advice about my mining venture. In the first place I may tell you that I have found the man who owns the shares. He is here in Victoria with his family. He is desperately poor. A hundred dollars if offered would be a great temptation. I would give more — $500 if necessary."

"The property you told me of the other day is valuable, is it not?" I asked.

"Yes — that is to say, we think it is. You know that mining is the most uncertain of all ventures. You may imagine you are rich one day and poor the next. It was so with my husband. He came home one day and said, 'We are rich'; and the next he said, 'We are poor.' This Maloney mine looks well, but who can be sure?

"When I came here I thought that if I found the man with the shares I could get them for a song. I may yet, but my dear child tells me that he has seen here a man from Grass Valley named Barclay, who is a friend of that shareholder, and," she added, bitterly, "perhaps he has got ahead of me. I must see the man at once and make him an offer. What do you think?"

"I think that you might as well save yourself further trouble. By this time the shareholder has been apprised of his good fortune."

"What!" she exclaimed, springing to her feet and transfixing me with her eyes. "Am I, then, too late?"

"Yes," I said, "you are too late. Forbes knows of his good fortune, and I do not think he would sell now at any price."

The woman glared at me with the concentrated hate of a thousand furies. Her great eyes no longer bore an expression of pleading tenderness. They seemed to glint and expand and to shoot fierce flames from their depths. They no longer charmed, they terrified me. How I wished I had left the door open.

45

"Ah!" she screamed. "I see it all. I have been betrayed — sold out. You have broken my confidence."

"I have done nothing of the kind. I have never repeated to a soul what you told me."

"Then who could have done it?" she exclaimed, bursting into a fit of hysterical tears. "I have come all this way to secure the property and now find that I am too late. Shame! Shame!"

"I will tell you. Barclay is really here. He knew of the strike as soon as you did. He is in love with Miss Forbes and followed the family here to tell them the good news. He is with the man at this moment."

"Curse him!" she cried through her set teeth

I left the woman plunged in a state of deep despair. I told her son that he should go upstairs and attend to his mother, and proceeded to the Forbes cottage. There I found the family in a state of great excitement.

Miss Forbes received me with great cordiality, and the mother announced that the girl and Barclay were engaged to be married, the father having given his consent at once. The fond mother added that she regretted very much that her daughter would have to abandon her literary career, which had begun so auspiciously through my discovery of her latent talent.

I looked at Barclay before I replied. His face was as blank as a piece of white paper. His eyes, however, danced in his head as if he enjoyed my predicament.

"Yes," I finally said, "Mr. Barclay has much to be answerable for. I shall lose a valued contributor. Perhaps," I ventured, "she will still continue to write from California, for she possesses poetical talent of a high order."

"I shall gladly do so," cried the young lady, "and without pay, too. I shall never forget your goodness."

I heard a low chuckling sound behind me. It was Barclay swallowing a laugh.

They went away in the course of a few days, and we corresponded for a long time. But Mrs. Barclay never fulfilled her promise to cultivate the muse, nor in her several letters did she refer to her poetical gift. Perhaps her husband told her of the pious fraud we practised upon her on Christmas Day, 1860.

What became of the Russian princess with the pretty manners, the white hands, the enchanting eyes, and the sweet "child" Bertie? They were back at Grass Valley almost as soon as Forbes and Barclay got there. From my correspondence, I learned that they shared in the prosperity of the Maloney claim, and that Mme. Fabre and her son returned to Russia to die among their noble kin.

An Ill-fated Family

Five brothers left Scotland for the Pacific Northwest, but there would be no pot of gold for the unfortunate family.

Early in the summer of 1860 the keel of a sidewheel steamer of light draught was laid in Victoria harbour. The vessel was designed expressly for navigating the waters between Victoria, Harrison River and Hope. The greatest care was bestowed upon her construction, and one of the most experienced shipbuilders on the Pacific Coast came from San Francisco to superintend the work. As the vessel was fashioned into shape her elegant lines won general admiration.

She was meant to have speed, and, with this object in view, engines and boiler of special design and great capacity and strength were ordered from Glasgow before the keel was laid. It was intended that the vessel should be ready for service by the fall of 1860, but there were several mishaps which prevented the trial trip being made until a year later. When the hull was nearly completed the timbers on which it rested gave way and crushed three men. One died; the other two lived. One of the latter, Richard Brodrick, was permanently lamed and carried the marks of the accident to his grave.

When the time came for launching the vessel she was christened the *Cariboo*. But instead of gliding off she stuck on the ways and had to be jacked foot by foot to the water. Her engines and boiler, which should have reached here in the summer of 1860, did not arrive until the spring of the following year.

The owner of the *Cariboo* was Captain Archibald Jamieson, an experienced navigator, who had gone early to Oregon where he commanded steamers that plied on the Columbia River. Archibald was a brother of Captain Smith B. Jamieson, who commanded the already mentioned Fraser River steamer *Fort Yale* when the vessel's boiler exploded three and a half months before the *Cariboo* was ready for service. On the ship that brought the *Cariboo's* machinery from Glasgow was a younger brother, James Jamieson, the baby of the family, as he was called. He was a tall, stalwart young Scotchman of about twenty-four, had learned the trade of engine-building at the works where the *Cariboo's* machinery and boiler were made. Being also a marine engineer, it was proposed to give him full charge of the machinery after a few trips had been made. An engineer named William Allen, who had been a long time out of steady employment, was temporarily appointed as chief engineer, with James Jamieson as assistant.

About the middle of July, the *Cariboo* made her trial trip and developed great power and speed. She was then despatched to Harrison River via Fraser River, returning with a cargo of white pine. The *Cariboo's* performances gave satisfaction, and her owner, who was also commander, was much pleased with the craft.

While the *Cariboo* was taking on cargo and booking passengers for her second voyage, in company with three or four other young fellows, I went into a restaurant. The waiter who took our orders was well known to me. His name was Paul De Garro, and despite his menial employment here he belonged to the nobility of France. His fellow-countrymen always told me that he was a count who had been exiled from France by Napoleon III when that monarch seized the throne and proclaimed himself Emperor. History records that barricades were erected in the streets of Paris by the populace, who were mowed down by the new Emperor's cannon until 50,000 lives had been lost and the empire firmly established on the blood thus shed.

Paul De Garro was among those who opposed the new regime. In consequence, he was exiled with many others to California in 1851. He came to Victoria in 1856 to visit the Catholic Bishop Demers. The Bishop had acquired a printing press, with a small quantity of French type, and two numbers of a weekly newspaper were got out in the French language. The title was almost as long as one's arm, for it was called *La Courier de la Nouvelle Caledonie.* Among the archives of the Catholic diocese there may be preserved a few copies of this, the first newspaper published on the British Pacific coast. Two years later, Mr. De Cosmos gave birth to the *British Colonist,* he printed the first and many succeeding numbers of his paper on the type and the antiquated hand-press that had been employed in the production of the *Courier.*

The Count was a very lugubrious-looking person. He could not accept his changed fortunes with easy grace or good temper.

As a waiter he was not a success, because he was condescending and patronizing and intensely irritable. If a guest objected to a dish with which he had been served, the Count would flare up and pick a quarrel with the objector. After a volley of "sacres" he would retire to the kitchen to sulk, and the proprietor, who was also the cook, would come into the restaurant and apologize for the impatience of the waiter-count, who could not forget that he had once lived in a palace and had himself been waited upon by "vassals and slaves." A peace having been patched up, the Count would pocket his pride and resume his duties until another complaint aroused his ire and started the ball again rolling in the wrong direction. To address him as "garçon" was a deadly insult, and he would never answer to any call that did not begin with "Monsieur" or "Count."

With all his brusqueness I rather liked De Garro, although a sight of his long, melancholy face often threw me into a fit of the blues. I always thought and said that he was entitled to sympathy rather than contempt, but many of the young fellows of the day did not share in that opinion. To them it was as good as a play to bait the Count until he lost his temper. One evening I sat in the restaurant reading a newspaper, and the Count, who had been drinking, was in a pleasant mood and quite talkative. He opened the conversation by asking if I had ever been in Paris. I told him I had not.

"Oh!" said he, "that is a place worth visiting. I lived there four years. I had plenty of money. My father's estates had not been confiscated then and I went everywhere — such parties, such balls, and, ah! such lovely ladies!

"Why did you not stay there, Count?" I asked.

"Stay there! What, live in the same atmosphere with that pig, that assassin, Napoleon? Never! never! He is a murderer — he killed my best friend. Attend to me while I tell you all. I went from Brittany to Paris. I was a student. I went to study medicine. In the same lodgings was a young woman — an art student — a handsome lady, bright, cheerful, good. I loved her when first I saw her and she loved me. We got well acquainted, and we were so happy we could have died for each other. I intended to marry her — God knows I did! — when I got of age, and had my parents' consent.

"Ah! My dear, sweet Estelle! Some day I will kill the man who killed you. Well, the President of France — that miscreant, Louis Napoleon — seized the Government and made himself Emperor. This was in 1851 — nine years ago. I objected. Although an aristocrat I was a Republican, too. I hated pomp and style. Barricades were thrown up and I served behind one. The troops came with cannon and swept away the barricades as if they were

Until completion of the Cariboo Wagon Road through the Fraser Canyon in late 1863, Douglas at the head of Harrison Lake was the start of the overland route to Cariboo. The *Cariboo* was designed to provide a service from Victoria to Harrison Lake.

The *Cariboo* was rebuilt as the *Cariboo and Fly* and served the B.C. Coast for over a quarter century.

made of paper. Estelle was with me. She loaded my musket and I fired it. Presently there was a rush of cavalry. We tried to stop it. No use, they poured over our breastworks and bayoneted or trod us under their horses' feet. Just as I fell I saw a cuirassier with raised sword strike poor Estelle on the head. I could not see what followed, but when I came to I saw my darling lying not far away, her lovely face smeared with blood that flowed from a ghastly wound on her head. I crawled to her. I raised her head in my arms. She was quite dead.

"Weak and wounded as I was, I supported that dear head until some men came to gather up the dead and wounded. They tore Estelle from me and threw her loved form into a cart with other dead bodies. I saw her no more. I was sent to a hospital, where I slowly recovered. I was told afterwards that the dead were interred in a common pit and destroyed with quicklime. Fancy that fate for dear Estelle, my love, my darling — to be eaten up with lime! When I was well, a decree of banishment was read to me and hundreds of others, and we were sent to California. From there I came here. I live with only one purpose — to return to France some day and strike down Louis Napoleon. When Estelle shall have been avenged I will die happy. I feel, I know, I shall see her again in the other world."

As the Count ceased to talk the fire died out of his eye, his face resumed its customary lugubrious expression, and the entrance of a customer who wanted a meal interrupted a conversation which was never resumed.

The Cariboo gold fields at that time had begun to attract public attention, and thousands from all parts of the world prepared to go thither. Victorians shared in the interest and among others Count De Garro was smitten with a desire to try his luck. Accordingly, he resigned his position in the restaurant and engaged passage on the *Cariboo* for Harrison Landing. The steamer was announced to sail at midnight on the 1st of August.

I was at the wharf at the hour set for sailing. I saw De Garro pass on board. He was accompanied by a huge black retriever, which was his constant companion. I wished the Count good luck as we shook hands in a farewell that was doomed to be our last on earth. Although steam was up at midnight, the Captain had not put in an appearance. Long afterwards I learned that he had a presentiment of evil and wished to remain in port till the next day.

From the wharf I walked to my room to bed, but could not sleep. A little clock on the mantel struck one, and then half-past one, and still I tossed from side to side. Sleep, although wooed with ardor, would not come to me. I was possessed with a strange feeling that an indefinable, horrible something was about to occur. Every little while I could hear the *Cariboo* blowing off what seemed to be "dry" steam in long-drawn volumes and disrupting the night air with the shrill notes of her whistle for miles around.

At last I heard the "cher-cher-cher" of the paddles, and then I knew that the *Cariboo* was off. I listened to the beat of the wheels for a few minutes; they grew fainter and fainter as the boat seemed to approach the entrance of the harbour. "Now," I thought, "I shall get some sleep," and I turned over on my side. Suddenly, a rending, tearing, splitting sound fell upon my ears. The "cher-cher-cher" ceased instantly, and the house shook as from the convulsive throb of an earthquake. The little timepiece on the mantel, which had just chimed two, trembled, reeled and stopped, as if affrighted by the shock. In an instant I comprehended what had happened. The *Cariboo* had blown up!

I was quickly dressed and rushed outside where the first streaks of dawn had begun to illuminate the eastern sky. As I hurried towards the waterfront I could hear the little bell on the Hudson's Bay Company's wharf ringing an alarm as if a fire were raging in the town.

I went to the wharf, and impressed a boat which I found tied to one of the piles and rowed out to the harbour mouth. The dim light of approaching day enabled me to discern the late beautiful craft lying a helpless, misshapen mass and drifting with the tide. A few lanterns were moving fitfully among the ruins. The upper deck had fallen in and the lower deck had been blown to pieces. Fortunately, the bottom was unimpaired, and as the wreck did not sink it was towed into a little cove and anchored there for safe keeping.

In the water at the side of the steamer we found the dead body of James Jamieson, the second engineer. I examined the corpse closely, and discovered that while one eye had been blown entirely out, the remaining eye was intact. It was staring with an expression of horror and alarm, showing that just as death claimed its victim he was aware of the grim messenger's presence, but too late to avert his fate. Captain Jamieson had disappeared, nor was any trace of him found for many days, when the sea gave up his mutilated form.

Henry Gray was the Fraser River pilot of the *Cariboo*. He had just left the captain at the wheel and gone into a room adjoining the wheelhouse to trim the binnacle lamp when the boiler burst. Gray fell with the ruins of the upper deck into the hold and escaped with a few bruises, but the captain, standing not three feet away, was taken. A passenger stood at the side of the boiler, conversing with the second engineer. When the steam and smoke had cleared the passenger found himself near the spot where he stood when the explosion occurred, while the engineer had been killed.

The bodies of the chief engineer and mate were found among the freight. They must have died instantly. Pieces of the boiler, the iron of which was of unusual thickness, were picked up on the boat and a few fragments were found on the shore. What remained of the shell of the boiler was deposited on the beach near the tragic scene.

I searched among the ruins for Count De Garro, but he was nowhere to be found, although the mattress on which he slept, saturated with blood, was shown me. The steward said that De Garro took his big dog into the room with him. As we conversed the dog made his appearance, having been picked up while swimming in the water, into which he must have been blown by the force of the explosion. The animal bounded at once to the spot where his master had last slept. Stretching himself on the mattress, he snapped at all who approached. He refused food and friendly overtures, even from me with whom he was well acquainted, but lay there growling and moaning. He was lariated at last and dragged ashore. For many days he haunted the wharves and the restaurant where the Count was latterly employed. Finally, he disappeared and was never seen again. The Count's mangled body was brought ashore one day, one of the six people killed in the disaster.

The coroner's inquiry clearly established that the cause of the explosion was too little water in the boiler. When the steam was blown off in vast volumes the boiler was emptied, then when the water was turned in it fell on red hot plates with the natural result.

The Jamieson family was a fated one. There were originally six sons, five of whom came to the Pacific Coast. One of the brothers was lost when a sternwheel steamer went over the falls on the Willamette River in 1857. Smith was lost by the explosion of the *Fort Yale* in 1861. Archibald and James were killed on the *Cariboo*, and a fifth brother lost his life by the explosion of the steamer *Gazelle* in Oregon. Thus perished five out of six of as "braw laddies" as ever left a Scottish home to seek fortune in a new world.

The *Cariboo* passed into the hands of Captain Frain, by whom she was renamed the *Fly*. The Marine Department objected to the change, but permitted her to be called by the double name, *Cariboo and Fly*. Captain Frain owned the steamer *Emily Harris* and employed both vessels in freighting coal from Nanaimo to Victoria.

One day in 1874 two Indians came ashore at Salt Spring Island in a boat. They reported that they formed part of the crew of the *Emily Harris*, and that the boilers of the vessel had exploded and the captain was killed. The story was not believed. Many have always thought that the Indians murdered the captain and sank the steamer. Nothing, however, was ever revealed to support this theory.

The *Cariboo and Fly* ran for a long time on the Coast as a cannery tender, but what eventually happened to her I cannot say.

Gravestone in Victoria's Quadra Street Cemetery for three of the five Jamieson brothers who died in Pacific Northwest steamboat mishaps.

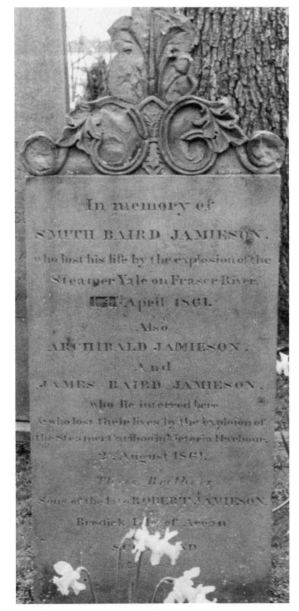

Only when Old Jackson's will was read
was the truth revealed about

The Saint and the Sinner

Why did everyone refer to him as "Old Jackson"? All the other boys on Yale flat were known as "Bill," "Jack," "Sam," or "Pete." Surnames were seldom used or needed. Christian names abbreviated answered all purposes for identification, reference or receipt. If there were half a dozen fellows in the camp with the same prefix, then some striking characteristic of manner, gait or speech was tacked on to designate which man was meant. But this man Jackson was never called anything except "Old Jackson."

If he had a baptismal name I never knew it — at least, not until I saw him sign his full cognomen under peculiar and painful circumstances. He was not old either — scarcely thirty — but he had a grave, quiet, absorbed way with him. He had come through with his own train of fifty or sixty pack animals from California. He had driven them across the then trackless Bad Lands of Montana and the sage brush of Washington Territory, into the Okanagan.

Jackson owned the train and, as the world went then, was regarded as rich. He brought with him a number of packers and armed men who were desirous to trying their luck at the Fraser River mines, then lately discovered. On their 1,000-mile journey the party had severe encounters with the natives. They lost two men and two were wounded. The dead men were buried in shallow graves after a rude burial service had been read over them. The wounded Old Jackson insisted on bringing along. He cast away the freight that two of the mules bore on their backs, substituting for the packs stretchers on which the poor fellows reclined. The average day's journey of a pack train is fifteen miles. To relieve the wounded, Old Jackson reduced the day's journey of his train to ten miles and pitched camp each day early in the afternoon.

Other pack trains from Oregon overtook and passed Jackson's. His assistants grumbled. They were anxious to test the new diggings and argued that unless greater speed was put on, all the rich claims would be taken up and the whole country would be under ice and snow before they should reach the Fraser. But Jackson was firm. He would not make haste while the wounded men were incapable of helping themselves. To abandon them would be to ensure their speedy death at the hands of the savages, who, thirsting for human gore and scalps, hung like wolves on the flanks of the train. Some of his force deserted and joined other trains; but Old Jackson crawled along at the ten-mile gait. It was not until late in September that he reached the Fraser and found that the packers ahead of him had disposed of their flour, beans, and bacon to the miners and traders and that the market was glutted with supplies of all kinds. He did not complain, but stored his goods at Lytton and Yale and sent his animals out to grass on the Thompson. A few of them died, but the humanity of Old Jackson saved most of his train, and the wounded men as well. When the packers who had passed him on the plains reached their journey's end, their animals were so run down that they were unable to withstand the rigors of an interior winter, and hundreds died from exposure.

Alvarez, a rich Mexican, brought to the country 125 loaded mules. He stored the goods at Yale, and then proceeded towards Hope, sixteen miles lower down the Fraser River, where he proposed to winter the train. He swam the animals through the ice-cold current and built huge fires on the bank, where the mules as they emerged from the water were rubbed down. All but three of these valuable animals, chilled through and through, died in a few hours. Jackson's animals passed through the winter in good shape, and the men who had condemned his slowness now applauded his judgment and humanity. He placed the train on the trail between Yale and the Upper Fraser and made heaps of money during the following two years.

Old Jackson was a very peculiar man. He was better educated than most of the men of his vocation, and his was a silent, unobtrusive personality. Often he would sit for hours in a group around a bar-room stove when his mind seemed far away. He never uttered a word or joined in the conversation until he was appealed to when, having replied in monosyllables, he quickly relapsed into silence. He drank little, swore not even at a refractory mule, and gambled not at all, but he read a great deal. I do not know where or how I got the impression into my head, but I always looked upon Old Jackson as a man who, like most silent men, although slow to anger, would be a dangerous character if once aroused.

This idea was confirmed on a dismal winter evening when a number of persons, to escape the pitiless pelting of a storm, had congregated for warmth about a huge red-hot sheet-iron stove in Barry's Saloon. Among the company on that evening was an elderly American who was known to his companions as "Judge" Reynolds. It was given out that at one time in his life he had been a man of some influence, that he had dispensed justice, and that, which was still better, in his earlier days he was an honest lawyer.

One this particular evening the Judge, who was much the worse for liquor and was in a talkative mood, was relating to the assembled miners an incident in his California career. To illustrate his story the old man rose to his feet and swung his long arms about after the manner of a political demagogue, while the "boys" who sat around listened with wide-open faces to the stream of eloquence that issued from his mouth.

The Judge had reached one of his flights of half-drunken oratory when the front door of the saloon was thrown violently open and a blast of piercing wind tore into and through the room. The company turned towards the door and saw standing there the figure of a man of medium height, his garments covered with snow. A Mexican sombrero was drawn over his eyes and his whole appearance was that of one who had travelled a long distance through the pelting of that awful tempest.

As he stamped on the floor to relieve his boots of the weight of snow that had gathered upon them he threw a keen glance around. Then he removed the slouch hat which half-concealed his features. One look into that face was enough for me. It was a face on every line of which was stamped the mark of sin and ruffianism. The man who sat next to me shuddered as he whispered, "It's Tom O'Neil!"

The name was one that had inspired terror in many hearts in California and Texas, and the appearance at Yale of the man who answered to it was regarded as an evil omen. I had never seen the man before, and I felt I would not die of grief if I should not see him again. While this thought was running through my mind the desperado, still holding his hat in his hand, advanced towards the stove. Room was made for him as he came forward, and he soon had a choice of half-a-dozen chairs. Having selected one he threw back his overcoat, and after another glance around the group, remarked:

"I walked up from Hope today. It's sixteen mile, I hear, but seems to me as it was a hundred." He paused for a moment as he held his open hands towards the stove to warm them, and then continued: "What did I came for? A picnic? Not much. I come for a man."

A shudder ran through the group.

O'Neil, who didn't seem to notice the agitation his words had caused, went on as if talking to himself:

"Yes, I'm after a man — leastwise, he's what some people calls a man. He threw dirt at me in Californy, and I've followed the varmint here to make him scrape it off. His name is — let me see, what's his name? Oh! yes, his name's one Reynolds — Jedge Reynolds he calls hisself, I reckon — a tall, big man what has a red nose and is much given to chin music. Perhaps none of you fellows don't know the man when you see him."

I stole a glance at Reynolds. He had ceased to talk and had fallen back in his seat when O'Neil appeared at the door. As I looked I saw him cowering in his chair with his hands before his face, apparently trying to reduce his figure into as small a compass as possible.

"Yes," said O'Neil, "he's my meat when I finds him. Do you uns know what he did to me? He sentenced me to the chain gang in Stockton for six months. Wot had I done? I only put a bullet into a man's leg as had refused to drink with me. He couldn't a-treated me much wuss if I'd killed the man. I hear he's here. Does any one know a man hereabouts which his name's 'Jedge' Reynolds?"

No one answered.

O'Neil keenly scanned the group again, and his eye swept along until it fell upon the quivering form of the old man.

"Wot do you call that objeck? Give it a name!" he snarled, pointing to Reynolds. "Seems like he's got the chilblains."

Still no answer.

"Then I'll take a look for myself." Rising from his seat the ruffian drew the old man's hat from his head and cast it on the floor.

I looked at Reynolds. His face was the color of pine wood ashes, and he trembled like a leaf as he raised his hands imploringly.

With a cry like that of a wild beast at the sight of its prey O'Neil sprang forward and clutched Reynolds by the throat with one hand. With the other he drew a Colt six-shooter from its holster, cocked it and pointed it full at the other's head.

"My God!" cried Reynolds, pleadingly. "Tom — oh! Tom, you would not murder me. Say you would not, Tom. Oh! say it's all a joke, dear, good Tom. Say you don't mean it — that's a good boy. I'm an old man, Tom. Look at my gray hairs and spare me."

"Curse ye," foamed O'Neil, "yer had a lot of mercy on me, didn't yer. Yer put me in prison and ruined my prospeks for life.

I've followed yer fer a thousand mile, and now I've got yer."

"Oh! oh!" wailed the old man, piteously. "Let me go this time, Tommy, dear boy. You don't mean to kill me, do you? I always said you were a good boy at heart, only you were misled. You would not harm a hair of my poor old head, would you, Tom? Just think what an awful thing it is to kill a human being —especially an old man."

O'Neil raised his pistol again and pointed it full at his victim's head. Reynolds sank on his knees to the floor, grasped his assailant's feet, and, as he grovelled there, continued to pray for mercy.

"No," cried O'Neil. "You've got just half a minute to say yer prayers."

"Tom! Tom! dear Tom," wailed Reynolds. "Make it a minute —give me sixty seconds."

"Yer'd better hurry," vociferated the coldblooded wretch. "There's only a quarter of a minute left." Reynolds burst into tears and fell over backwards. As he lay there he feebly pleaded. "Someone pray — pray as my poor old mother used to pray — for me."

"Time's up!" roared O'Neil. He raised his weapon and took deliberate aim at the prostrate form. While this scene was being enacted I sat speechless and rooted to my chair. I had seen death in many forms, and imagined that I was proof against any horror. But the prospect of seeing a man's brains blown out in cold blood was too much for me, and indeed, for the whole company, since no one moved, but just gazed helplessly on the scene.

"One two, th—," shouted the desperado.

Then a strange thing happened. Like a flash the muzzle of the pistol was struck upward and the ball intended for Reynolds lodged in the ceiling. The next instant I saw O'Neil in the grasp of a man. He struggled to release himself, and a volley of oaths poured from his wicked mouth. The two men fell to the floor as in a death grapple, the intruder beneath. O'Neil, whose pistol had fallen to the floor, reached for his bowie knife, but before he could draw it from its sheath the under man turned him over and pinned him to the floor. In another moment O'Neil was relieved of his bowie knife (his pistol having been taken possession of by one of the bystanders), and was allowed to rise. Panting for breath, he sank into a chair.

Then I saw that the victor was Old Jackson! He had interfered in time to save Reynolds' life.

Reynolds left the river the next day and Tom O'Neil apologized to Old Jackson and became one of his best friends. But the taint of ruffianism was too deep in Tom's system to be entirely eradicated by one discomfiting circumstance, as the following

Pioneer surgeon Dr. John S. Helmcken diagnosed Old Jackson's fatal illness. Dr. Helmcken arrived at Fort Victoria in 1849 and practiced for over 60 years. He died in 1920 at 96. His house, beside the Provincial Museum, has been preserved and is open to the public. The first part was built in 1852 and is considered the oldest residence in B.C. which is essentially unchanged.

Below: A mule pack train similar to Old Jackson's at Barkerville. The 400-mile trip from Yale took about a month, with only three trips usually made during a season.

incident will clearly illustrate.

There was a little negro barber at Yale who was known as "Ikey." He was a saucy and presumptuous creature, with a mischief-making tongue in his head. Into Ikey's shop one day entered Tom O'Neil.

"Barber," quoth he, "I want yer to shave me."

"Yeth, sah," said Ikey, "take a seat."

"And barber," continued Tom, drawing a revolver and placing it across his knees, "if yer draw so little as one drop of blood I'll shoot yer."

The barber, fortunately, did not cut the vagabond, and so escaped with his life. In narrating the incident Ikey said: "If I'd a cut that man ever so little I made up my mind that I'd cut his throat from ear to ear. It would ha' been my life or his'n, and I was shore it wouldn't a been mine."

One afternoon about two years subsequent to the occurrences I have narrated above, I strolled slowly along Yates Street in Victoria. About the last person I expected to meet was Old Jackson, and yet as I neared the corner of Government Street I almost ran against him.

"I was looking for you," he remarked, "all day yesterday. I got down the day before from Yale and wanted to see you badly."

"What's the matter?" I asked.

"I've sold my packtrain and intend to go to California. I was too late to catch the steamer and shall have to wait three weeks before another chance will come for getting away. I am very ill today. My left side feels as if there was a lump of ice inside of me. I went to Dr. Helmcken this morning and he told me I must go to bed and stay there, that I am threatened with pneumonia."

Together we walked to the Hotel de France and went to his room. He breathed heavily and was very weak.

"I feel that I shall never get over this trouble," he said. "I don't think that I shall live long. I have some property and I want you to get me a lawyer so that I may make my will."

I summoned George Pearkes. After two or three interviews the terms of the will were arranged and the lawyer took the paper away and deposited it in a safe. From that day Old Jackson never left his bed, and the doctor said that his trouble was quick consumption.

One day, about a month after the will was drawn, Jackson handed me a letter and asked me to post it. I saw that it was addressed to "Thomas O'Neil, Esq., Yale, British Columbia."

Jackson must have detected a look of surprise in my face, for he remarked in an explanatory manner:

"Tom's not such a bad fellow, after all. After you left the river we became good friends and I got to like him. This letter tells him to come right down, for I want to see him before I die."

The letter was mailed about the 10th of December, and two days before Christmas Tom O'Neil walked into the hotel. He had changed but little. If anything, he was more villainous-looking than before, and had the same swaggering, devil-may-care air that I had observed when I first saw him in Barry's Saloon in Yale. He was shown to the sick room. In the evening I saw him at dinner. His manner was quieter and more subdued, and I thought — only thought, mind you — that his eyes were red as if from crying.

The next day we were told that Jackson was sinking and might go at any moment. O'Neil was constantly at the sick man's bedside, and in a rough but kindly way did all he could to relieve the distress of his friend. But the end drew rapidly near. Just before daylight on Christmas morning I was summoned from my room by a message that Old Jackson was dying and wished to say goodbye to me. I responded at once.

O'Neil stood at the head of the bed looking down on the face of the sufferer. His eyes were suffused with tears and his whole frame shook with emotion, which he found difficult to control. I could not understand his agitation. Was it assumed or real? Could it be possible that this desperado — this murderer at heart, if not in deed, this social outcast — was it possible that his wicked mind was open to generous impulses and emotions?

Mentally I responded, "No; he is humbugging the friend about whom he has woven a strange spell that death alone can break." I was scarcely civil to O'Neil. He looked out of place in a death chamber, at least in a death chamber that he had not himself by one of his murderous acts created.

"He's goin' fast," O'Neil whispered as I entered.

The sick man opened his eyes and gazed long and fixedly at Tom. Then he turned his head feebly to me and said in a low voice, "Be kind to him when I am gone."

I was startled. There was something so extraordinary in the request, coming as it did from a man whom I had learned to respect for his goodness of heart and bravery in staying the hand of the ruffian for whom he now pleaded.

"Yes," Jackson continued, "be good to him. He never had a chance. His mother died when he was a small boy and he ran away and came West to escape a cruel step-mother. It was not his fault if he grew up bad. He never meant to do half that he threatened to do. If he has done wrong he has suffered for it. I have forgiven him and if the rest will forgive him he'll do better."

O'Neil, in a paroxysm of sobs, flung himself from the room.

"Will you promise me?" urged the dying man.

"Yes," I said, most reluctantly. "I will do what I can."

A smile stole across his face. He tried to extend his hand, but it fell back on the counterpane. "The will," he said, "the will will explain all."

The first gleam of dawn on that Christmas morning was welcomed by the glad ringing of a little bell. The sound fell on the ear of Old Jackson as he lay dying on his bed. He half raised himself and then fell back on the pillow.

"George," he feebly moaned, "Do you hear? It's our old schoolbell ringing. It's time to go home."

He paused for a moment and then went on: "I'm choking for air. Oh! Give me a chance. Open — please open that window and let in the air."

Someone raised the window and then there was borne in on the early breeze the sound of voices singing.

As the voices rose and fell in soft and gentle cadence the sick man raised himself on his elbow, the better to listen. When the voices ceased the bell resumed its call.

"Yes, George," said Old Jackson. "Let's get our books and go home. Dear mother will be waiting." He turned on his side and faced the wall. When the bell ceased to ring Old Jackson had indeed "gone home."

The next day Old Jackson was placed in the Quadra Street Cemetery. After leaving the cemetery we repaired to the hotel, where Mr. Pearkes read the will. It ran something like this:

"I give and bequeath to my brother, George Jackson, sometimes known as Thomas O'Neil, all my property, real and personal, that I die possessed of, the only stipulation being that he shall erect a suitable stone over my grave, recording thereon my name, age and birthplace, and try and reform.

"JAMES JACKSON."

The property amounted to between $7,000 and $8,000 in gold, all of which the bank paid over to O'Neil the following day. He returned to the Mainland and resumed his evil course. Three years later, at the diggings on the Big Bend of the Columbia River, he was voted a dangerous nuisance by the miners. A mule was procured, a rope passed around the animal's body, to which the desperado's legs were tied, and he was sent out of the camp with instructions never to return on pain of death. He was never heard of again, by me at least. Perhaps he perished in an attempt to reach civilization.

Afterward I visited Quadra Street Cemetery. The desperado did not erect a stone to the memory of his brother. The grave is unmarked and undistinguishable.

Why B.C. Lost the San Juan Islands

It became known as the "Pig War," and though there was no shooting, B.C. lost to the Yankees.

In the fall of 1858 there arrived at Victoria a tall, dark, haughty looking Irishman with a military bearing. He gave evidence, in the absence of one of his eyes, of hard usage on some battlefield. The gentleman's name was Major De Courcy, and he claimed to have seen service in the Crimean War, then Britain's latest unpleasantness. He brought high recommendations as to character and fitness, which he presented to Governor Douglas. It was not long before he was enrolled on the commission of the peace and was sent to San Juan Island as magistrate.

That Island had long been a preserve of the Hudson's Bay Company, who raised pigs, sheep and horned cattle thereon, while the company's servants took unto themselves wives and raised many children. A number of British and American farmers, attracted by the fertility of the soil, also settled there, and quite a community of both nationalities soon began to grow up. Previous to the advent of Major De Courcy as Justice of the Peace, the two races had mingled in perfect harmony, and neighborhood disputes that sometimes arose were settled in a way satisfactory to all parties.

I am not aware that Britain's rights to sovereignty over San Juan and adjacent islands had been seriously questioned before 1859. Certainly no overt act was committed and no claim officially submitted by the United States previous to that year. Shortly after Major De Courcy made his appearance on the Island, an American settler stole or confiscated or shot for trespass a fine Berkshire hog belonging to the Hudson's Bay Company. The magistrate, on complaint being made, haled the offender before him, and either imprisoned or fined him.

The disputed San Juan Islands between Vancouver Island and Washington. The British claimed that the Islands were theirs, so did the U.S. The British proposed establishing the middle channel as the boundary but the U.S. disagreed. Finally, the two sides agreed to let Emperor 1 of Germany arbitrate the dispute. In 1872 he awarded all of the Islands to the U.S.

In disposing of the case De Courcy was unnecessarily severe in his strictures on the American settlers, and threatened that if necessary the whole power of the British nation would be invoked to punish them. One would have thought that a grave question of state was involved — that the rights of the Government had been attacked and were imperilled — whereas the trouble was all over a pig, worth four or five dollars. But momentous events have often flowed from small circumstances. Not to travel too far from home for an example, the great territory of Oregon was lost to the British Crown because the salmon of the Columbia River will not rise to the fly!

The brother of the Earl of Aberdeen, the British Premier in 1846, commanded a warship on the Oregon Coast. The territory was then in dispute. One day the Premier's brother started out for a day's fishing, but coax as he might he failed to induce a single salmon to rise. Disgusted, he wrote home to his brother: "A country where the salmon will not rise to the fly is not worth a d——." So it came that Great Britain withdrew her claim and the whole of Oregon and Washington Territory, which were hers by virtue of prior occupation, passed under American rule. Between a pig and a salmon, Britain's interests were sadly undone on the Pacific Coast.

The American residents, regarding the treatment of their fellow countryman as an act of tyranny, and affecting to believe that the Island was American territory, appealed to General Harney, who was then in command of the U.S. forces on Puget Sound. Harney despatched Captain Pickett with a small force, and instructed him to land on the Island, lay claim to it in the name of the American Government, and resist any attempt that might be made to dislodge him.

Briefly stated, the contention of the Americans was this: the line which defined the boundary between the British territory and that of the United States ran on the west side of San Juan and the other islands, known as the San Juan group. The British held that the line ran on the east side of the group, and that all the islands west of the line were British territory.

The news of the invasion of the island by an American force created much excitement when it reached Victoria, Washington and London. A fleet of warships was detached from the Chinese station, and ordered to proceed with all despatch to Esquimalt and there await orders. At one time there were twelve warships in Esquimalt harbor, and a thriving business was driven by Victoria merchants.

Everyone here expected that there would be war. Governor Douglas, who was a man of strong feelings and unimpeachable loyalty, denounced the invasion as an outrage, and claimed the right to use force in expelling the invaders. Admiral Baynes, who was in command of the fleet, favored the adoption of temporizing measures and declined to allow the fleet and the men under him to retake the Island without instructions from Downing Street. In due course instructions came, and were to the effect that until the two Governments had had a conference matters were to remain as they were.

General Winfield Scott and Governor Douglas, representing their respective Governments as commissioners, met at Port Angeles. They arranged for joint occupation of the Islands until the dispute had been composed by arbitration. A British force was then landed, and the two garrisons maintained friendly relations until, fifteen years later, Emperor William of Germany, acting as umpire, decided that the American contention was correct. The Islands passed under the control of the Washington Government.

Long before the termination of the "war" — in fact, while affairs wore their most ominous aspect — De Courcy was withdrawn from the Island. It was felt that his life was not safe there. He came to live again at Victoria, where he grew exceedingly unpopular because of his overbearing demeanor. He sometimes sat on the Police Court bench with Mr. Pemberton and administered a sort of Jedburgh justice upon Indian offenders and whiskey sellers. He seemed to delight in inflicting heavy penalties for light offences.

The *Colonist* often rapped him over the knuckles, and in the somewhat crude vernacular of the day referred to him as a "snob and a Bashi-bazouk." It was said that De Courcy commanded a company of those notorious Turkish irregulars, the Bashi-bazouks, during the Crimean War, and that he lost his eye while engaged in a village raid. This may have been a libel, because, as the story will show, De Courcy, although a decided martinet, was deficient in neither courage nor ability.

Among the officers of the fleet was a Captain De Courcy. He belonged to the English branch of the family — the De Courcy of whom I am writing being of the Irish branch. Now it so happened that at that time there was no love lost between the two nationalities of the distinguished line. One day the brace of De Courcys met on Government Street in front of the Colonial Hotel. Approaching the English De Courcy, the Irish kinsman said:

"Am I addressing Captain De Courcy?"

"You are," was the reply, short and sharp.

"I, too, am a De Courcy," said the Irishman.

The Englishman raised a monocle, screwed it into his eye, and surveyed his distant relative from boot to hat with a malig-

General Winfield Scott, above, Commander-in-Chief of the U.S. Army and James Douglas, Governor of the Crown Colonies of Vancouver Island and British Columbia. They agreed to a joint occupation of the Islands with 100 soldiers each, thus averting an impending war.

The British camp in the 1860s. Today both the British and the American Camps are preserved as U.S. National Historic Parks.

nant look. "The h— you are," he said, and strode off.

With the outbreak of the U.S. Civil war in 1861, De Courcy saw his opportunity. He got together his effects and left for the States. Arriving at Washington, he presented his credentials and was made a colonel. His first engagement was at the siege of Vicksburg, a Southern stronghold which was beleaguered by General Grant. De Courcy showed so much bravery on that occasion that he was made a brigadier-general. His men, before going into action, hated him. He was so tyrannical and exacting that they made up their minds to kill him at the first chance. But, as one of them told me, "The fellow was so brave and careless of his own safety and comfort that we could not harm him. With some of our generals it was 'Go on, boys!' With De Courcy it was

'Come on, boys!' for he was always first. He bullied and damned us, but he would not let us go where he would not go himself."

After the fall of Vicksburg, De Courcy was sent with his brigade to a Confederate fortress at a place called Cumberland Gap. He was instructed to invest the fortress, but to delay further action until the arrival of the commander-in-chief. Upon reaching the Gap, De Courcy detected the weak spot in the enemy's works, and at once assaulted the place with the result that it soon fell into his hands with many prisoners and all the munitions of war.

The next day, upon the arrival of the commander-in-chief, De Courcy was cashiered and dismissed from the army for disobedience of orders and presumption. Was there ever a greater act of ingratitude done by a jealous superior officer? De Courcy did what Lord Nelson did with impunity — won a great victory by disobeying orders. Nelson was loaded down with many honors. De Courcy was dismissed in ignominy. Different nations have different ways of recognizing ability and pluck.

It may be mentioned as an extraordinary circumstance that the Southern commander at Cumberland Gap was Pickett, the captain who invaded San Juan Island and set De Courcy's authority at naught. At the outbreak of the war Pickett resigned from the Union Army and joined the Southerners. He was made a general and was one of the bravest of the brave among the Southerners. Pickett was not captured at the Gap, being absent at Richmond when De Courcy took the place.

Pickett, when I knew him, was about thirty-five years of age, of medium height, a handsome, dashing fellow, with yellow hair, which he wore very long, after the fashion of the Vikings, whom he very much resembled. He rose to great distinction in the Southern Army, and died at Richmond after the war was over.

De Courcy went back home. It was understood while here that he was a distant connection of Lord Kingsale, the Premier Baron of Ireland, but so remote were his chances of attaining to the peerage that it never entered the head of any one to speak of his high possibilities. But fate often decides things in a way that is foreign to our anticipations and expectations. One after another the immediate heirs to the Kingsale peerage died off and cleared the path for Major De Courcy. Then one day the old earl died, and our disagreeable Victorian, the former Bashi-bazouk, the originator of. the San Juan "war," being next in line, succeeded to the title and estate. The peerage is one of the most ancient in Great Britain, dating back to the twelfth century. Major De Courcy, or rather Baron Kingsale, died in Italy. As for the San Juan Islands, they still fly the Stars and Stripes instead of the Canadian flag.

When the leader of Victoria's social elite
was snubbed because she had "A Past," the
consequence surfaced at

The Mayorial
Banquet — or Brawl?

One morning in February 1860, there appeared in a Victoria paper's advertising columns a notice:

"At the instance of Mr. John Colber a writ was yesterday issued from the Supreme Court against Dr. Balfour of this city.

The writ alleges slander on the part of the defendant and the damages asked are heavy."

The appearance of the advertisement set all tongues wagging. Every man and woman and, for the matter of that, every child who was old enough to understand what a suit at law meant, was anxious to know just what it was all about. Colber was a sturdy Scotsman, Writer to the Signet (which, I believe, means the same as barrister here) of about forty and had a wife some ten years his senior. When asked for an explanation he shook his head, and said, "Go and ask the doctor — he knows."

The doctor, when appealed to, professed ignorance of having given cause for the action and appeared to be as much puzzled as the community in general. In the burning desire for information, Mrs. Colber was asked. She was a little Englishwoman, of quick, nervous action, black snappy eyes, and a tongue — as old Willis Bond, the famed colored orator, expressed — "dat cuts bof ways like a knife."

Mr. and Mrs. Colber had arrived at Victoria by ship from Australia in 1859. They had some money and built themselves a small shack which answered the double purpose of a law office and a residence. Mrs. Colber immediately began to assert herself as a social leader. She gave little teas (then quite an innovation — and tea was not the only beverage served) which the "best"

The Victoria waterfront in January 1863. The ball which started the controversy was held in the Hudson's Bay Company's warehouse, at right behind the paddlewheel steamer.

people attended. At one of them it was decided to form a sort of social guild for the purpose of ascertaining who was who — dividing the sheep from the goats, weeding the society list, so to speak — and admitting only those whose records were unimpeachable to the circle. It was felt that in the hurry and bustle of strangers arriving and settling here, some very undesirable persons had succeeded in imposing themselves upon society. They were carrying their heads high when, were the truth known, they should hang them very low.

About this time a ball was arranged to be held at the Hudson's Bay Company's warehouse, which then stood at the foot of Yates Street. It was used for storing salmon in barrels pending the annual sailing of a Company's boat, the *Princess Royal*, for London. When the ball was arranged the vessel had taken all the salmon on board and the warehouse was empty. After liberal applications of soft soap and water to destroy the ancient and fishlike smell that hung about the place, and the draping about the walls of sails and flags from the ships, the room was made presentable and a goodly number of invitations were sent out.

There were very few ladies then resident in Victoria. Families were scarce, and a child of tender years was regarded as rare. Now it happened that to the social club of which Mrs. John Colber was the self-elected leader was assigned the task of selecting the ladies who should be invited to attend the ball. The guild met and appointed a secretary to whom was given the duty of writing the invitations, and an executive committee to check the list was also appointed. In due course the cards were issued. To the surprise of many, the names of Mr. and Mrs. John Colber were not among the elect. A day passed, two, three days, and still no cards for the Colbers. Then arm-in-arm (which was the way married and engaged persons walked at that time), the Colbers proceeded to investigate. They were very angry, and the sharp tongue of the lady cut like a two-edged sword.

The unfortunate secretary was the first object of the slighted woman's wrath. After much persuasion and many threats, the secretary explained that she had been instructed by the committee not to issue an invitation to Mr. and Mrs. Colber. To the president of the committee the pair next proceeded. In that lady they encountered a foewoman who was worthy of the visiting lady's tongue. The word-battle must have been interesting. It was said that Mrs. Colber got the worst of the combat. She left the place, supported by her husband, and in an hysterical condition.

As I have explained, the outcome of the visit was the issue of a writ for heavy damages against the husband of the president of the Executive of the Social Guild. What provoked the action I never knew positively. In was reported, however, that a gentleman from Australia had known Mrs. Colber while there and said that she had a "Past." Now to say that a person has had a Past is not actionable in itself. We have all had Pasts. Some of us would gladly erase the record from the slate and think of it no more if we could. But to say that Mrs. Colber had a Past and to strike her name from the list of eligibles because of that Past was decidedly actionable.

The ball came off and proved very successful. There were ladies present, but the gentlemen outnumbered them six to one. The moment a lady entered the dancing apartment she was pounced upon, so to speak, and her "card," which was written upon a half-sheet of note paper, was filled almost at once. A young American who accompanied me to the ball got one dance the whole evening and I fared little better, the naval officers bearing off all the honors. The costumes were rich and varied. Of course, the enormous crinoline was much in evidence. In sympathy with hoops the gentlemen wore baggy trousers, wide from the hips to the ankles, where they suddenly narrowed and were drawn closely in. There was about as much fit in trousers then as there is in pyjamas now. Looking back, I can recall nothing so grotesque as the male and female costumes of that day — and yet we thought them graceful and fetching and altogether lovely!

The supper was all that could be desired. I remember that Governor Douglas, Captain James Reid and other heads of families, with their lovely young daughters, were present, and that the Governor and other gentlemen made very pretty speeches, in which they referred to the company in a pleasant manner. Admiral Baynes, then in command on the station, and his staff were also present, and he, too, made some appropriate remarks. The affair passed off pleasantly and the cocks were crowing their welcome to the rising sun before the company dispersed.

"Do you intend to push the case against the doctor?" I asked Colber one morning.

"Yes," he exclaimed with emphasis, "to the bitter end — to the death, if necessary."

"Won't you accept an apology?" I continued.

"No," chimed in his wife. Her eyes snapped with excitement. "Never — never! If he lay dying and asked me to forgive him I never would."

Within two weeks from the date of that conversation Dr. Balfour was dead. It seemed that he worried much over the action and saw no way out of the suit except by flight. A little brig called the *Florencia* was loading for Chili. On this brig Dr. Balfour, to escape the action, secretly took passage. Off Cape

73

Flattery the brig encountered a fearful gale and sank. Amongst those who were swept off and never seen more was poor Dr. Balfour. He was truly followed to the bitter end — to death.

The passing of Dr. Balfour gave quite a shock to the little Colony, for the deceased was well liked, and the social position of the Colbers was rather lowered than heightened by it. Shortly after the sad event, the couple became involved in bitter warfare with W.B. Smith, owner of a brick building on Government Street, the lot extending to the line of Colber's lot on Langley Street. The latter always insisted that the Smith fence encroached three or four inches on their lot. The wordy wars were many and numerous.

The active spirit in the Smith establishment was a young clerk named Hicks. After the passage of numerous fiery epistles, Mrs. Colber cowhided Hicks on Yates Street and was fined $25. Next Hicks and Colber met and Hicks pulled his antagonist's nose, for which luxury he paid $25. Then Colber printed a card in which he referred to Hicks as a man who had been publicly cowhided. Hicks retorted with a letter in which he referred to Colber's nose as having been tweaked on the public street.

In the absence of a theatre, the controversy created the keenest amusement to the residents. While one party would pat Hicks on the back and advise him to keep it up, another section would tell the Colbers to give it to Hicks. On one occasion Hicks found a dead cat in Smith's backyard. Naturally supposing that his enemy had thrown it there he hurled it over the fence into Colber's yard. It chanced that the little woman with the fiery temper and snappy eyes was engaged with a tape-line and an Indian boy in measuring the ground to find how many inches of land had been taken possession of by Smith. The defunct feline landed full on her head, giving her a severe shock, and causing her to imagine that a wild animal had leaped upon and was about to devour her.

Loud screams brought the husband to the spot. After he had soothed his wife, he seized the dead cat by the tail and darted round the corner to Smith's store. Hicks was standing in the doorway. He was a bit of a dandy and very vain. As Colber approached, Hicks tried to escape. But he was overtaken, and Colber nearly wore the animal out on the head and shoulders of his enemy. The town went wild with delight. They had watched the clash between the two forces for some weeks. The comic side of a controversy always appeals most strongly to the popular mind, so the funny incident of the cat and the use that was made of it took the public by storm. Nothing else was talked of for many days and the "Tsick him, boy!" tactics were continued by the friends of both.

The boom consequent on the discovery of gold in Cariboo struck Victoria in 1862. The buildings were of insufficient capacity to accommodate one-tenth of the people who came to Victoria to make this the starting-point for their long journey to the mines. Hundreds of the newcomers pitched tents on vacant lots, and the streets were crowded with people from every part of the world.

Goods were in such demand that the steamers from San Francisco could not carry one-half the freight that waited shipment. Real estate in Victoria rose rapidly in value, and nearly everyone became a speculator. The Colbers bought two lots on Pandora Avenue and sold one of the two immediately afterwards for a sum equal to that which they had paid for both.

In the summer of 1862 the city of Victoria was incorporated. Thomas Harris, a leading business man and a generous, public-spirited citizen, was unanimously chosen mayor. Amongst the town councillors elected was John Colber who, in spite of his unpopularity, received the highest number of votes and consequently became senior councillor. The Prince of Wales (later King Edward) attained his majority on November 9, 1862, and a public holiday was proclaimed. A procession was formed and, headed by a band, marched through the streets. In the afternoon there were races at Beacon Hill Park, and in the evening an illumination of the public buildings, the mayor's and several other private residences. For the evening a banquet had been arranged at the Lyceum Hall.

About two hundred guests appeared at the table, over which Mayor Harris presided. In the gallery were a number of ladies who had assembled to "see the lions fed," and who were served with wine and sweets. Full justice was done to the excellent menu and the usual patriotic toasts were drunk with enthusiasm. Then followed a number of toasts of a local character and all went pleasantly.

There was not the slightest reason to suspect that a storm cloud lurked in the air — that the peaceful scene, almost pastoral in its serenity and calmness, was soon to be changed. It became a roaring, seething maelstrom of disorder and confusion where men would lose their heads and shout and strike out wildly, and fair women's screams would add to the din. The red rag of the occasion was a toast to "The Mayor and City Council." The Attorney-General having proposed it, the Mayor responded for his office in a pretty little speech which was applauded. When Councillor McKay rose to respond for the City Council he found himself forestalled. Already on his feet was John Colber.

"Mr. Mayor," he began, "as senior councillor the duty devolves on me to reply to the toast of the City Council."

Victoria's first mayor, Thomas Harris, presided at the banquet celebrating Victoria's incorporation in 1862. By then the ramshackle wooden buildings of the gold rush were being replaced by brick structures like those below on Government Street.

"You are out of order, Councillor Colber," said the Mayor.

"Oh, no, I'm just as in order as senior councillor."

"But you are not down for this toast. Councillor McKay is, and I can only hear him."

"Begging your pardon, Mr. Mayor," replied the senior councillor, while a sweet smile swept over his broad face. "The duty devolves on me to answer, and I'll not shirk my duty. It is a source of great gratification —"

Cries of "Order," "Order," "Sit down," "Chair," arose. The glasses danced and jingled in response to vociferous thumping on the table and the fireworks began. The noise was deafening, but high above the din could be heard the tempestuous voice of sturdy John Colber as he repeated over and over again the words, "Mr. Mayor, Mr. Mayor."

Rising higher still the shrill soprano of an excited female rent the disturbed air as it called out, "Stand your ground, John! Don't be put down, John! Fight for your rights, John!"

Guests who turned their heads in the direction whence the female voice came saw a little woman with a very pale face and snappy black eyes leaning half over the front of the gallery. She was swinging her arms frantically as she called to her husband at the top of her voice. The woman was Mrs. John Colber.

On the floor of the hall the disturbance grew more and more pronounced. One man, a little fellow named Briggs, managed to burst through the throng and reach Colber.

"John Colber," shouted he, "you're a hass — a feckless hass!"

"A little louder, Mr. Briggs," cried John, with a seductive smile.

"I say you are a feckless hass, John Colber."

"Actionable, Mr. Briggs, actionable. You hear him, gentlemen? I'll make a note of those words."

"Look out, Billy!" cried a voice from the crowd, "He'll sue you and get them three lots of yours."

Billy turned as white as a ghost and shot out of sight.

The cries of "Sit down" and "order" continued to resound through the room, but Colber refused to sit down or be sat upon.

The Mayor at last lost patience, for the Governor and his staff, naval officers and other dignitaries had left the room. His Worship cried out, pointing to Colber, "Will no one remove that nuisance?"

At this a rush was made for the senior councillor. A dozen hands were laid upon him. A mob of thirty men closed in upon the "nuisance" and threw him bodily out of the hall. As he struggled to release himself, the high soprano of his wife was again heard as she rained an orange, an apple, a cake and a plate upon the guests below. Then she dashed down the stairs. Throwing her arms about her husband, she led him towards their home, calling down heaven's maledictions on his assailants as she went.

The Colbers decided to erect a brick dwelling on their remaining lot on Pandora Avenue. It was to be a double house and two stories in height. When the walls were nearly up a difficulty presented itself. The Jewish community resolved to build a synagogue adjoining the Colber lot on the west. The synagogue was to be bigger and higher than the Colber mansion and would throw it into the shade. The Colbers would not submit to be over-shadowed in that way, so they added another story to their structure. "From the roof of which," said the lady, "I can always command a fine view."

During construction Mrs. Colber was frequently present. One day as she was climbing up a ladder "to get a view" from the unfinished roof, a little unslacked lime fell from above and entered her eyes. The pain was excruciating. She walked home and means were employed to remove the stuff. But relief came too late. The lime had slacked in her eyes and the light had gone out from those snappy organs forever. From that day till the day of her death, the unfortunate woman was totally blind! The building, which was erected at a greater elevation than had been originally intended, still stands. Other eyes have feasted on the view to be had from the roof, but the lady for whose pleasure the elevation was increased never saw again!

The devotion of John Colber to his blind wife was marked and touching. Her temper, never of the sweetest, grew worse under her great misfortune. But Colber put up with everything and was accustomed to lead her with exemplary tenderness and patience through the streets for an airing or to and from church.

The last time the couple came before the public was in the summer of 1867. As a barrister, Colber had sued Dr. John Ash on behalf of John Nicholson, a well-known contractor, for work done at or near Sooke. Judgment was rendered for about $1,500. The money was paid into the barrister's hands on Saturday, too late to be deposited in the bank. Colber put it into a sort of apology for a safe, in reality only a wooden box enclosed in sheet iron about one-fourth of an inch thick.

On Sunday evening the pair went out for a stroll and were absent about an hour. On their return they found that the iron and wood box had been cut through with a cold chisel and every dollar was gone. No trace of the thieves was ever discovered. Thus Mr. Nicholson, after winning his case, lost his money.

A little later Mr. and Mrs. John Colber's names appeared in the passenger list of an ocean-bound vessel. I heard that she died in Australia and that he went back to Scotland.

The Duel

"Have a care," G.B. Wright warned the young man. "My experience of steamboat acquaintances is rather unfavorable!"

Early on July 19, 1858, in company with some twelve hundred other adventurous spirits who had left California to try their luck in the Fraser River gold fields, which were then attracting the attention of the world, I landed from a rowboat on the waterfront of Esquimalt town. We had followed in the wake of some 20,000 other gold seekers.

The old steamer *Sierra Nevada*, in which we voyaged, was overladen with freight and passengers, and it seemed a miracle that she survived the heavy winds and waves that beset her path. We were nine days on the way and the discomfort was great. Hundreds of the passengers — men, women and children — unable to secure berths or sleeping accommodations of any kind, lay about on the decks and in the saloons in the abandon of despair and hopelessness. Only a few escaped an attack of seasickness. I was among the fortunate ones. Having voyaged much in earlier life I was seasoned to all conditions of weather.

I had a stateroom in which there were three berths. One of these was occupied by G. B. Wright, who afterwards rose to eminence on the Mainland as a pioneer merchant and road builder. He was a bright, energetic man at that time, young and chock full of enterprise and ability. The remaining room mate was a young Englishman who said his name was George Sloane.

He was very intelligent, and having lately left college in England, was fond of quoting Latin and Greek phrases and reciting poetry, which he did very well. In the next room was an American named Johns, whom I had known at San Francisco, another American named Crickmer, also a San Francisco acquaintance, and a third young man who called himself John

Gustavus Blin Wright, inset above, the author's travelling companion on the
Sierra Nevada. Wright became a prominent businessman and built about
one-half of the 400-mile-long Cariboo Road from Yale, above in 1868, to
Barkerville. The church at lower left beyond the flagpole is St. John the
Divine. Built in 1860, it is still in use, the oldest church in B.C. still on its
original foundation.

Below: A stagecoach on the Cariboo Wagon Road. Service from Yale to
Barkerville started in 1864, the journey taking 52 hours — weather
co-operating. The route of the original Wagon Road is generally followed by
today's highway.

Liverpool. This last person was English, he said. He was of a jovial disposition, smoked a good deal and drank brandy from an earthen gallon jug. He could tell a good story, and Wright and I — the others being prostrated with seasickness — used to lean over the rail and listen to his fund of anecdote and adventure. Sometimes he would make us laugh immoderately, and at others our hearts would be stirred with pity as he related some pathetic story of his early life.

About the fifth day out a woman passenger died, and on the evening of the same day she was buried at sea. Captain Blethen read the funeral service as the corpse, sewed in canvas and weighted with iron, was shot over the side. I have often wondered how any of us escaped with our lives. The condition of the ship was abominable; the water was bad, there was no attempt at sanitation, and the stench from the hold was unbearable. The food was wretched, and so the brandy in Mr. Liverpool's jug was the ebb-tide mark long before we sighted Cape Flattery.

On the sixth night the head wind stiffened to a fierce gale. In spite of all we could do to reassure the wretched people on board, many resigned themselves to their fate and few expected to see land again. That night two men, who had come aboard healthy and strong, succumbed and were buried at sea the next morning. The afternoon of the seventh day was bright and warm. The wind died away, the sea calmed and the steamer began to make fairly good time. The sick people gradually crawled from their hiding places, looking wan and wretched enough, but loud in the expression of their thanks that they had come through the tempest with their lives.

I presently observed a young woman of eighteen or twenty who had struggled from below. She was pale and thin, and bore on her face a look of wretchedness and misery. I got the impression that when in health she must be very pretty, and I recall that she had a wealth of dark brown hair, a pair of glorious hazel eyes and regular features. She sat watching the gulls as they rode on the crests of the billows, and I thought I had never seen a prettier picture. I was tempted to speak to her but, as I was on the point of advancing, a burly figure pushed by me and engaged her in conversation. Their tone was low, but they seemed to be acquainted. Mr. Liverpool, for it was he who had put my amatory "nose out of joint," hung about her till bedtime. When Liverpool passed me on the way to his stateroom, I asked about his pretty acquaintance.

"Yes," said he, "she is pretty. Her name is Bradford — Miss Bradford. She is very unfortunate. Her mother was the lady who died and was buried the other day, and she is alone in the world. I knew them in San Francisco. The mother kept a boarding-house on Powell Street. They were on their way to open a boarding-house in Victoria, but of course that is all over now and she will have to go back."

The next morning I was early on deck and there sat the pretty girl with the hazel eyes again watching the gulls as they skimmed over the surface of the waves. The morning was warm and pleasant, the land was in sight, and the assurance of the Captain that next day we should be at Esquimalt brought the color to many pallid cheeks.

At this moment Sloane, advancing with difficulty along the crowded deck, reached the girl. He held in one hand a cup of tea and in the other a plate on which were an orange and some biscuits. As he was about to hand the articles to the girl, Liver-pool, who was standing near, took the cup and plate and himself handed them to Miss Bradford. The girl never looked at Liver-pool, but she flashed her beautiful orbs full in Sloane's face, and thanked him in a low, sweet voice. Sloane, who seemed some-what disconcerted at Liverpool's interference, hesitated a mo-ment and then walked to where Wright and I were watching events.

"You seem," said I, "to be making progress in that direction."

"Well, you see," he replied, "I was up at dawn, and you know the saying about the early bird, etc. I have had a long talk with her. Since her mother is dead she has no friends left except a brother at San Francisco, and she intends to go back by this very boat. She has no money either. It was all in her mother's purse, and when she died money and purse disappeared — stolen by some miscreant. She is very intelligent, very sweet, and, oh, of such a grateful and confiding nature. She told me everything about herself and I know all about her and her belongings."

"Have a care," said Wright. "My experience of steamboat acquaintances is rather unfavorable."

"My dear fellow," rejoined Sloane, "there are acquaintances and acquaintances. This girl is as good as gold. What do you say? Let's start a subscription for her. I'll give $20."

The idea was adopted, and in about ten minutes Sloane was on his way back to the girl with a considerable sum — I think about $100. I accompanied him. Liverpool stood behind the girl's chair, conversing with her in a low tone.

"Miss Bradford," began Sloane, speaking very slowly and very low, blushing like a schoolboy the while, "I have brought you a small sum as a loan from a few of your fellow passengers. You can repay it at your leisure."

He was about to place the coin in the girl's outstretched hand when Liverpool wrenched the money from his grasp and tossed it overboard.

"Look here!" he exclaimed, "this girl is not a beggar, and if she stands in need of money I have enough for both."

Sloane was speechless with indignation. His eyes blazed with anger. "You d——d cad," he began, and then recollecting himself he paused and bit his lip.

"Go on," said Liverpool; "I'm listening."

"Miss Bradford," said Sloane, ignoring Liverpool, "do you countenance — do you approve of this man's conduct?"

I looked at the young woman. Her face had assumed an ashen hue; her lips were colorless and her beautiful eyes were filled with tears. She half rose and then sank back and seemed about to faint.

Sloane still held the reins of his passion and refused to let it get away with him, but he was livid with repressed rage.

"Do you," he at last managed to say to Miss Bradford, "do you approve of this man's beastly conduct? Has he any right to control your movements, or to say what you shall or shall not do? Please answer me, and if he has a claim upon you I will go away and trouble you no more."

The girl rose from the chair and was about to reply when Liverpool's right arm shot out and his fist struck Sloane full in the face between the eyes. Sloane staggered, but he did not fall. In an instant he recovered his balance, and, quicker than it takes to tell it, he seized Liverpool by the throat with one hand while with the other he delivered about a dozen smashing blows in rapid succession upon his antagonist's face and body.

It was all over in half a minute. Liverpool, his face streaming with blood and half dead from the choking and pounding, dropped into the chair which the girl had vacated as she fled from the scene. I took Sloane away and got a piece of raw meat from the steward to bind over his eyes, which were both blackened.

The next morning the passengers landed at Esquimalt from the steamer in small boats (there were no wharves). Having seen nothing of Liverpool and Miss Bradford since the affray, I began to hope that we had heard the last of them — not because I was not deeply interested in the fair creature (for I may as well confess that I was), but I feared if the two men came together again there would be a tragic outcome. We walked to Victoria in the afternoon and found the town crowded with gold seekers. Houses were few and the whole townsite was covered with miners' tents. There must have been 10,000 people there.

Crickmer, Johns and I had brought a tent and a good supply of food. Sloane we invited to camp with us. Although he was a casual acquaintance we liked him from the start, and his plucky display of science when he beat John Liverpool endeared him to us. The first night we slept on a bed of fir boughs. In the morning we built a fire, and Crickmer, who was a good cook and had been accustomed to camping out, began to prepare the morning meal. Presently he came inside and, lowering the flap of the tent, said, "Boys, who do you think are our next door neighbors? Guess."

We all gave it up, and he exclaimed, "Liverpool and Miss Bradford occupy the next tent."

Sloane sprang to his feet with a furious oath, exclaiming, "If he has wronged that girl I'll kill him."

"Nonsense!" said I. "When you've been on the Coast a little longer you will not make such a fuss about people you chance to meet when travelling. What is she to you, anyway?"

Crickmer and Johns took the same view. We extracted from Sloane a solemn promise that he would not speak to Miss Bradford if he met her and that he would not notice Liverpool under any circumstances. Unfortunately, he could not keep the promise.

As we concluded our conversation the flap of the tent was raised and a broad, good-natured face appeared at the opening.

"Boys," the face said, "I've been here a month. I know all about everybody. I live next tent on the north, and anything I can do to help you, ask me. I want to warn you. I saw a bad San Francisco man pass here a moment ago. He disappeared in one of the tents. Keep a close watch tonight."

Little did we think at the time that the bad man was Sloane's steamboat antagonist.

We ate our meal in silence, and then walked to Government Street to enjoy the sights and sounds that are inseparable from a mining boom. About the noon hour we ate luncheon at the Bayley Hotel. The luncheon cost each man a dollar, and for a glass of water with which to wash down the food each paid John C. Keenan, who kept bar at the Bayley, fifteen cents. Water was scarce and just as dear as Hudson's Bay rum. As for baths — well, there was the harbour. A bath of fresh water at that time would have been as costly as the champagne bath.

We returned to the tent about five o'clock in the evening and set about preparing our dinner of bacon and beans and flapjacks. Presently, Liverpool and Miss Bradford appeared. The girl seemed ashamed and, hurrying into their tent, did not appear again.

Johns and I had arranged to meet Wright at seven o'clock and attend a minstrel show at the Star and Garter Hotel. So we sauntered down the road to keep the appointment. What happened after we left the tent was told us by Crickmer amid tears and sobs, for his was a very nervous and emotional temperament. He said that as he and Sloane sat about the campfire smoking their pipes after we had gone, Liverpool came out of his tent. His face bore the marks of his severe punishment. Sloane's eyes were also black. Liverpool, who was accompanied by three or four evil-looking men, his voice quivering with passion, said to Sloane, "I demand satisfaction for the injury you have done me."

Sloane rose slowly to his feet and, keeping his eyes full on the other's face, replied, "I have done you no injury."

"You have," said Liverpool, passionately. "You insulted my wife by offering her money, and you beat me like a dog when I refused to let her take it."

"I did not know she was your wife," said Sloane.

"She wasn't then, but she is now. I married her this morning," returned Liverpool.

"What do you want me to do?" asked Sloane.

"I want you to fight me — now, here — this minute. Get your pistol."

"I have done you no wrong, and I won't fight you. Besides, I have no pistol," said Sloane.

"Then I'll brand you as a liar and coward, and will kill you, too."

"Take care, Liverpool," said Sloane. "Don't go too far."

"Go too far! Why, man, if anything I can do or say will make you fight I'll say and do it. Take that," and the ruffian spat full in the other's face.

"Give me a revolver!" exclaimed Sloane, enraged beyond control. "I'll fight you. But it must be with the understanding that after we have fought I shall be troubled no more."

"Yes," said Liverpool, his every word seeming to carry a hiss, "after you have fought I shall be troubled no more."

The awful significance of this remark was realized later on.

Crickmer said he clung to Sloane and implored him not to fight. But the Englishman's blood was up, and he struggled like a wounded tiger. Two of Liverpool's companions dragged Crickmer, who was little and frail, aside and threatened to shoot him if he interfered further.

A crowd of miners had been attracted to the spot by the loud talking, and one of them unbuckled his waist strap and handed Sloane a six-shooter.

"It's a good one and never misses," the miner said. "Do you want a second?"

"Yes, will you act?" asked Sloane.

The miner consented. Liverpool chose one of the evil-looking men as his second, and the principals and seconds, followed by a gang of several hundred campers, repaired quickly to an open space. Beneath the shadow of the English Colonial Church

"Gentlemen, are you ready?"

ten paces were stepped off and the men took their places. Liverpool, winning the choice of position, stood with his back to the sun, a manifest advantage.

As for Sloane, the glory of the departing sun shone full on his face. The music of birds was in his ears. Sweet wild flowers bloomed about him. He took all these in with a sweeping glance, and for a moment turned and gazed at the old church. Perhaps a vision of his childhood days, when a fond mother directed his footsteps to the House of Prayer, swept across his mind. The next instant he faced his adversary, dauntless and cool.

"Gentlemen, are you ready?" asked one of the seconds.

"Ready," both responded.

"Then — fire!"

There were two reports, but only one bullet found its billet. With a loud cry of agony Sloane fell forward. He had been shot through the heart.

The sun sank behind the Metchosin Mountains, and the chill evening breeze sighed a requiem through the branches of the tall pines. The midsummer moon rose in all its splendor over the tops of the trees, and its soft rays fell upon Something lying there still and cold — Something that a short while before was an animated human being, full of hope and promise and chivalry. Now, alas, dead to all things earthly. The scene was deserted by every living thing, and the dew of heaven, like angels' tears, had fallen on the stricken youth's form and bathed his face and hair ere the police appeared and bore the body to town.

As Johns, Wright and I came out of the show place, two hours later, we saw a stream of excited men and women passing along. "A man has been shot dead," said one of the passers-by. We followed the crowd to the corner, and with some difficulty elbowed our way into a deserted building.

Our feelings may well be imagined when we saw our late steamer acquaintance and tent mate, whom we had left a short time before, lying dead on the floor. An inquest was held and a verdict of "wilful murder" was returned. But the surviving principal, the seconds and Miss Bradford were gone. No man could be found who would acknowledge that he saw the duel. All who had not run off were struck suddenly blind, deaf and dumb.

When we came to prepare the poor youth for the grave, the man who had given us the warning as to the presence of a bad character helped. We had asked a Presbyterian minister to read the service. But we found a gold medallion of the Holy Virgin and the Child suspended by a chain about the neck of the corpse, so the Bishop of the Catholic mission read the funeral service of his Church over the remains. Nothing was found in the dead man's travelling bag to indicate who he was. We only knew that he was a brave young English gentleman who had been done to death by a bloodthirsty ruffian through a mistaken idea of what constitutes honor.

And John Liverpool and Miss Bradford — did I ever hear of them again?

Yes. John Liverpool was in reality "Liverpool Jack," a noted California outlaw. Immediately on his return to San Francisco he murdered the mate of a British ship and was executed with neatness and despatch by the authorities there. Crickmer, whose terrible experience while here prompted him to take the next boat for home, wrote me some years later that he often saw the girl with the wealth of hair and glorious eyes flitting along the pavements at night like an evil spirit.

So ends the story of British Columbia's first and only duel.

Fate was the Hunter

Druggist James Moore saved the depressed woman's life, but later only her husband could have prevented her terrible tragedy.

The early servants of the Hudson's Bay Company at Fort Victoria resided behind the palisades and within the fort, or clustered in one-story cabins of hewn logs, white-washed inside and out, and built without the slightest regard to architectural effort or sanitation. The men who came here in pursuit of gold in 1858 erected their places of business along the line of Yates and Wharf Streets, and disposed of their goods on a strictly cash basis. The thoroughfares, which were wagon tracks in summer, in winter became quagmires in which horses and drays often stuck and men sank to their knees. There were no street light, sewers, water — none of the conveniences that now contribute to make life enjoyable. Many of the merchants occupied rooms above or behind their warehouses and raised families of children blooming with health and vigor. Bachelor merchants not only slept in their offices, but cooked there as well.

On one occasion I went into a Wharf Street store to buy a flask of quicksilver, which was sold wholesale at $2 a pound. The merchant and I had a long conversation as to prices. He made several attempts to cut the argument short by manifesting a desire to retire to the room in the rear, which served in the treble capacity of office, bedroom and kitchen. Each time I detained him by raising some new point and presently my nostrils were assailed with the odor of something burning. The merchant took the scent at the same moment and, cutting a sentence short, made a wild rush to the kitchen. In a moment he emerged holding a frying pan in his hands.

"There!" he exclaimed, as he gave me a malignant look, "while I've wasted my time talking to you my sausages have been burned to a crisp!" He threw four blackened sausages into the street.

One of the most picturesque characters in the down town district at that time was James Moore, a druggist, who dispensed drugs and chemicals at A.J. Langley & Co.'s. Mr. Moore was an Englishman of rather retiring manners. He was amiable and good-natured to a fault, never known to turn his back upon a glass of good brandy or rum; in which genial habit he was not alone. To his intimates he was known as "Jem" Moore; to mere acquaintances as Moore; to the general public as Dr. Moore.

As a druggist he had few equals, and as prescriptions were from $2 to $5, the profits were large and Moore earned the liberal salary that was paid him. Moore did not live at or near his place of business. Early in 1859 he had married a Mrs. Dewig, the widow of a German grocer, whose husband had left her a tidy little fortune. After the marriage Mrs. Moore hyphenated her name and had her cards printed "Mrs. Dewig-Moore." Several of Moore's friends ventured to address him as "Dewig-Moore," but the manner in which he received the innovation caused them to refrain from repeating the liberty. They returned to the more familiar, if less musical, appellation of "Jem" Moore.

"I want to be something more in the world than Mrs. Dewig's husband," Moore was accustomed to say. "I want to be known and appreciated for myself alone. I don't propose to have my personality buried in the Dewig grave and Dewig dug up and put in the front rank. Dewig is dead; let him rest. Moore's alive; let him live. If the widow of the defunct wants to carry the dead man's name on her card, well and good. It pleases her and does me no harm. But, by the gods of war, I refuse to be addressed in her dead husband's name, so don't call me by that any more."

Moore, as I have said, was a kind-hearted man and performed many acts of goodness. He was a most careful druggist, and no mistake was ever traced to him. With all his amiability he could be very firm when occasion required, as the tale I am about to relate will show.

One dark and dismal night the rain fell in great sheets and the wind roared over sea and land. It was December of 1861. Moore was on the point of closing for the night when the door swung back and a female figure was blown in. She was closely muffled up to protect her from the fury of the gale, and the lower part of the face was hidden behind a red shawl. In spite of the shawl, Moore could see that the woman was nice-looking, and that she had coal-black eyes that sparkled with what seemed to be an unnatural fire. Approaching the counter, the woman hesitated for a moment and then, allowing her eyes to fall, said in a faltering voice, "I want two bits' worth of laudanum."

Moore regarded her face for a moment with a suspicious air and asked, "What do you want it for?"

"I want it for the toothache."

"It wouldn't require so large a quantity as that. A few drops on cotton wool will do. Here, I'll put a few drops in the tooth."

"No, no, no," said the woman, shrinking away. "I must have two bits' worth. All my teeth are aching. Give it me and let me go."

Moore considered a moment. He felt certain the woman before him meant to commit suicide. If he refused to sell her the poison someone else might.

"Well," he said, "you may have the poison if you will promise to be careful in its use."

"Yes, yes," cried the woman, eagerly. "I promise."

Moore filled a small phial with a dark fluid, labelled it "Laudanum, Poison," and handed it to the customer. She almost snatched it from his hand. She threw down the coin and, with a smothered "Thank you," left the store as rapidly as she had entered it.

Moore gazed after her with a queer look, while a smile played about the corners of his mouth. Then he lighted a little candle and, placing it within a tin lantern (coal-oil was not then used in lanterns), banked the fire, closed and locked the safe (that was before combinations were invented), fastened the doors and sallied forth into the night. The feeble rays shed by the candle guided his footsteps along the muddy footpath (no boarded sidewalks then existed). He walked along Yates through the slop until he reached Government Street. The wind was holding high revel. Signboards creaked and buildings groaned and trembled before heavy blasts that tore fiercely through the little town as if anxious to sweep the place clean off the map. Moore's hat blew off, but he did not stop to recover it.

The guns of Fort Victoria frowned down upon him as if they were preparing to go off on their own accord and contest with the elements a right to a monopoly of the noise. The lonely wayfarer continued to pick his path slowly and was passing the palisades of the fort when the feeble rays cast by his lantern disclosed something that caused his kind heart to beat with alarm. In an instant he had recovered himself and, bending down, saw that the figure of a woman lay extended on the walk.

A glance showed that the prostrate woman was the one who had asked for the laudanum a short time before. He placed his hand on her shoulder and shook her gently. The woman moaned and, drawing the red shawl over her face, turned her back to the light.

"Come," said Moore. "Get up. This is no place for a human

On the left is the Adelphi Saloon at Yates and Government Streets. The Moore and Company store is three doors toward Wharf Street.

The guns at Fort Victoria which in 1862 frowned on James Moore as he tended to the woman who tried to poison herself. The Fort was totally dismantled by 1864.

being on such a night — and a woman, too."

"Oh! go away and let me die," the woman replied, in pitiful accents.

"Let you die! No indeed," said the druggist. "Why should you die? What have you done to make you wish to die?"

"Oh! I've taken poison — laudanum," she said. "In a few minutes I shall be dead."

"But you have not taken poison," persisted Moore.

"I have, indeed. I bought it at Langley's — two bits' worth. I swallowed it all and have laid down here to sleep. Oh! go away and let me die in peace."

"Woman," said Moore, "I am the druggist who filled your order. I did not give you laudanum. I gave you a small phial of weak paregoric, with a dash of ipecac to act as an emetic. If you wait till that kills you will live forever."

The woman sat up. In imploring tones she begged Moore to assure her that he had spoken the truth. No reply was necessary. At that moment the ipecac made its presence manifest in no uncertain way. When the woman had sufficiently recovered Moore assisted her to her feet. Her clothes were wringing wet and she trembled with cold and weakness.

"Have you told me the truth?" she again asked the druggist.

"Yes," replied Moore. "As God is my judge, I gave you nothing that would harm you. Now come with me to my home and my wife will look after you."

He half led, half carried the forlorn creature, who was too weak to resist, to his door. A blazing fire filled the hearth; a cold grouse flanked with a bottle of Pyramid beer and another of brandy stood on the dining-room table, set there for Mr. Moore's supper. Moore led the woman to an easy chair before the fire and poured out a generous drink of brandy, which he almost forced down her throat. Then he ran out of the room and aroused his wife.

Mrs. Dewig-Moore spoken broken English. She was eccentric, vain and silly on most subjects, but when it came to helping a woman in distress she was the best-hearted creature in the world. She almost dragged the stranger off to her room, where she gave her a hot bath, hung up her wet raiment to dry, and then put her to bed between blankets with a bottle filled with hot water at her feet. In the morning early the stranger awoke, arrayed herself in her garments, and would have left the house by stealth after penning a short note of thanks to her host and hostess. But they were on the alert and barred her. They made her partake of breakfast, which she did while grateful tears chased each other down her face.

They made no effort to gain her confidence and the woman

left after telling Mrs. Moore that her name was Wilmer and that she was married. Some days later the Moores inquired and found that the Wilmers had left and gone whither no one knew. They heard no more of the woman for a long time — nearly a year.

One afternoon in 1862, Mrs. Moore was called into her drawing-room by a message brought by the servant that a lady wished to see her. As she entered the room the visitor rose. She was tall and graceful, and well dressed in clothes of fashionable make and fine texture. Mrs. Moore paused in the act of extending her hand, for the lady seemed an entire stranger.

"You do not recognize me?" asked the visitor.

"No, I cannot remember to have seen you before."

"And yet," returned the lady with a smile, "you have met me before and have entertained me."

Mrs. Moore studied the face carefully and then shook her head. She did not recognize a line of the features.

"You do not recall my face?" the lady asked.

"No, I cannot call it to mind."

"Well, then, I am Mrs. Wilmer, whom your husband found lying on the street and brought here, and to whom you were so good. I have come to tell you that fortune has smiled upon me. My husband has made much gold at Cariboo. He is interested in one of the richest claims on Williams Creek. I have brought you this nugget as a gift to show how much we appreciate your great goodness to me when I needed your help." She handed Mrs. Moore a large lump of pure gold. Mrs. Moore at first declined the gift. But the lady insisted, and she finally yielded.

"Now," said Mrs. Wilmer, "you are entitled to an explanation of my strange conduct a year ago. My husband and I are English born. He is one of the best men alive when he refrains from the use of drink, but under that blasting influence he is a demon. On the night that I bought the laudanum he came home in a state of intoxication and struck me. I ran into the street and made my way to Mr. Moore's place. I fully intended to kill myself.

"When my husband found that I had gone he searched at once, for he really loves me. He searched for me all through that bitter night and when he got back to the house at noon he found me there. He took me in his arms and knelt at my feet. He asked my forgiveness a thousand times. He made a solemn vow on his mother's Bible to drink no more. He has kept his oath. I went with him to Cariboo. I cooked and baked and washed and kept boarders while he worked in the mine, of which he is part owner. Providence blessed our efforts.

We came down a week ago with nearly $5,000, and there is plenty of gold awaiting our return in the spring. We have sent

$3,000 to relatives in England and have given $100 to the Royal Hospital. We have enough left to keep us through the winter. I am a very happy woman, Mrs. Moore. Whenever I ask God to forgive my great sin, from the consequences of which the wisdom and foresight of your husband saved me, I always ask Him to bless you both."

Mrs. Moore was delighted to find that her visitor was the woman whom she had helped in an hour of deep distress. The women embraced with expressions of happiness and pleasure. Mrs. Wilmer then blushingly said to Mrs. Moore: "We have been blessed in another way," and she whispered something in her hostess's ear.

"No!" exclaimed Mrs. Moore. She was pleased, as ladies always are, to be made the repository of the most interesting secret that one woman can impart to another. "When?"

"In about a fortnight," returned Mrs. Wilmer. "Are you a mother?" she asked.

"No," said Mrs. Moore, "I am not so fortunate."

As Mrs. Wilmer rose to go Mrs. Moore promised to call upon her soon. Then the ladies parted, never to meet again on this earth.

A fortnight flew by, during which Mrs. Moore had almost forgotten the visitor and her strange story. Then one morning a paragraph in the *Colonist* brought the incident back to her mind with startling vividness.

The paragraph went on to relate that a Mrs. Wilmer, residing on North Park Street, had died under most painful and extraordinary circumstances. It was stated that she awoke in the middle of the night and found herself in immediate need of a doctor and nurse. She aroused her husband and he, dressing quickly, departed in search of both, whose services had been bespoken some weeks before.

I cannot recall the doctor's name, but Mrs. Charles Moss, a noted midwife, was the nurse. The doctor was not at home and the unfortunate man visited a saloon, hoping to find him there. In the saloon he encountered a number of lucky Cariboo miners who were celebrating their good fortune. Wilmer, after much persuasion, was induced to take "just one drink." He took another and another and was soon in a state of intoxication. He forgot his sick wife and the errand upon which he had gone forth.

Two days passed and on the evening of the third day he staggered homeward. He found the door locked, as he had left it. No smoke ascended from the chimney and no sound was heard from within. He knocked. There was no response. He opened the door and entered. In the uncertain light he stumbled over a prostrate form. He stooped, and with a cry of anguish and guilty despair he saw the body of his wife, clad in her night garments — cold as ice and stilled in death.

The wretched man rushed from the house and aroused the neighbors with loud cries of horror and remorse. Lights were brought and then was revealed a sight that would melt a heart of stone. The poor woman had fallen from her bed to the floor and she and her babe had died for want of those attentions her husband had been sent to procure. The dead woman's hands were battered and bruised as if she had pounded in vain on the floor to attract the attention of neighbors, one of whom remembered that he had heard cries two nights before but thought they came from the street.

As I bring this mournful chapter to a close, the day is spent and the sun has sunk to rest behind a glorious halo of golden mist. Twilight has deepened into darkness and night has draped its sable curtain over earth and sky. I lay down my pen and seem to see the figures I have sketched glide by in ghostly procession. The miserable conscience-stricken husband who totters and shakes like one suddenly stricken with palsy; the kind neighbors who wring their hands and sob, "If we had but known!"; the strong men who bear the remains of mother and child to the Quadra Street Cemetery; and the young curate who breaks down and weeps in the midst of the funeral service.

Then I hear the dull clods fall on the coffin that holds the remains of the dead woman with her tiny babe close pressed to her heart and happily oblivious forevermore to worldly wretchedness, poverty, neglect and inhumanity. I hear the solemn words: "Earth to earth, ashes to ashes, dust to dust" echoing through the churchyard.

Then the ghosts flit away into the dim Past, and are seen no more. I awake from my long reverie, and find myself seated in the gloom with only memory and this poor little story for my companions.

Jem McLaughlin's Transformation

Yale's bullying butcher became an outstanding citizen after his bruising encounter with the quiet-spoken hotel keeper.

There was much that transpired at Yale and, indeed, throughout the Colony of British Columbia that created a deep impression upon my young and ardent mind. Many things happened that cannot be written, that were of too horrifying a nature to be recalled now. There is, fortunately, a great wealth of reminiscent lore that can be and ought to be unearthed for the information, if not the instruction, of the present generation of men and women. No one who wishes to be regarded as a faithful historian can afford to disregard it.

Nearly every early resident of Yale, Vancouver and Victoria readily recalled the personality of Captain William Power. He amassed a fortune during the land boom at Vancouver and died a few years later. The Captain, who was an Irishman, was a splendid specimen of manhood and was an accomplished athlete.

I first met him early one sunny morning in August 1858, on the saloon deck of Captain Thomas Wright's sternwheel steamer *Enterprise*, as she ploughed slowly against the current on her way to Hope. I had risen early and was reading a book when I saw approaching me a tall, fair young man. He held in one hand what seemed to be a China mug. As he drew near he said: "I've been all over this precious craft looking for the steward. Do you know where he is to be found?"

I replied in the negative, adding that I was, like himself, a stranger on board.

"I want some hot water," he said. "I've travelled all over Europe and the Holy Land and have been on the Nile, but this is the first time I have found it impossible to get a cup of hot water to shave with. What do you use?"

I told him I used cold water.

"If I've got to use cold water," he replied, "I'll not shave at all," and he didn't for several years.

In the course of the day he introduced me to Mrs. Power, a bright young German lady, and we three became fast friends. Our friendship was maintained for many years, for they were an estimable couple.

We pitched our tents at Yale and Mr. and Mrs. Power opened an hotel on the flat. It was speedily regarded as the very best in town, and the couple soon had a full house. There was but one butcher shop in the town at that time. It was owned by a man named Carlyle. One Jem McLaughlin officiated at the block. He was a most desperate black-guard, both in appearance and action. He was a huge, bloated specimen of humanity and was generally filled to the throat with drink. When in that condition he was most abusive to his customers. He took a delight in placing before them portions that they did not desire or order, generally with the remark, "Take it or leave it," showing that he was aware that he possessed a monopoly of the meat business.

I had two or three tilts with the fellow, and every time was worsted because he held the key to my stomach. He insulted and bullied everyone, including Power, whose restaurant was at the mercy of the bloated butcher. He could cut off the supply of meat at any moment and put Power out of business. The language he used was fearful. He brow-beat women as well as men. He hated children and would often turn them crying away without the food they had been sent by their parents to buy. A poor dog that strayed into the shop afforded him the greatest joy and satisfaction, for if he could not reach him with his foot he would hurl a cleaver at him, once or twice with deadly effect.

A Scotchman named McDermott was the owner of a beautiful little terrier, his constant companion in all his prospecting tours. The little fellow ventured into McLaughlin's shop one morning to pick up scraps when the wretch struck him with his great cutting knife across the back, inflicting a wound that maimed the dog for life. The owner of the animal was furious. He seized his revolver and started for the shop to shoot the butcher. Friends intervened and induced him to give up his weapon, but he went to the shop and, addressing McLaughlin, said: "If I ever catch you on the other side of the line I'll kill you — kill you!"

"Go on out of this," shouted the butcher, "or I'll serve you as I did the dog."

"Very well," said McDermott, "I'll go; but remember, you will be my meat if I ever catch you on the American side."

McLaughlin fired a volley of words in defiance and the

Scotchman went away, reminding McLaughlin of his threat.

How we submitted patiently to the tyrannous conduct of the ruffian, even at the risk of losing our meat supply, I cannot imagine now. But we did, and most humbly. He led us captives to the block and decapitated us morally, if not physically. For a long time he ruled supreme. He was monarch of all he surveyed and keenly enjoyed his regal position. But one day he struck a snag, or, rather, a snag struck him. "The worm turned," and although worms are not generally supposed to have teeth, this particular worm had a good sharp set and bit the oppressor till he howled.

Down on the bar there lived a little English woman named Burroughs. She had two dear little children, a boy and girl, who were noted for their neat appearance on all occasions. Her husband had gone up the canyons in quest of gold, leaving wife and children in a small tent. A scanty supply of groceries and money which he left behind for their sustenance was exhausted and the family were reduced to great straits. The neighbors on the waterfront did all they could to help the woman, but they were generally poor, too. It was understood that Mrs. Burroughs was too proud to appeal for help.

Winter was approaching and the discomfort of occupying a tent in cold weather will be understood by those who have passed through that experience. The little woman had been a frequent customer at the butcher shop and had paid for what she got so long as her purse held out. Lately, she had fallen in arrears. One morning, when she asked to have an order filled, McLaughlin was in one of his worst moods. He had been revelling overnight and had lost heavily at the faro table. So when Mrs. Burroughs lined up with others in front of the block His Majesty addressed her in language something like this: "What do you want?"

"I should like to get a little more meat on credit for a few days. Mr. Burroughs will be here soon and he will pay you," she timidly said.

The wretch leaned on his cutting-knife and regarded the woman with a diabolical leer as he said: "Is there a Mr. Burroughs? Was there ever a Mr. Burroughs? I doubt it."

The hot blood mounted to the woman's face and painted it crimson. She fixed her eyes in a terrified stare on McLaughlin and her lips moved as if in remonstrance. But no words came from them. She leant forward on the block and then sank to the floor. She had fainted. Strong hands raised the thin, wasted figure (It turned out afterwards that for some weeks she had systematically lived on the shortest of short allowance so that her children might have enough to sustain them.) A low murmur of indignation ran through the line of McLaughlin's subjects who awaited their time to be served.

"Come on, now," roared McLaughlin, "and give your orders quick. I can't stand here all day. What do you want?" he asked, addressing the next customer, who, by a strange fatality, happened to be William Power.

An eye-witness told me afterwards that Power turned as white as a corpse when the wretch insulted Mrs. Burroughs, but he said nothing.

In response to the ruffian's question, he gave his order.

"You can't get what you want; you'll have to take what I'll give you. Do you hear that? Here's a piece of meat that's good enough for the Queen."

"It's not good enough for my table, anyhow, and I'll not take it," said Power.

"Then go without. Who's the next?" shouted the butcher. "Stand aside, will you, and give place to a gentleman?"

"McLaughlin," said Power in slow, measured words, "every time that I come to your shop I am insulted. This thing has got to stop. I don't care so much for myself and I could have stood it, but I do care for that poor little woman." He pointed to Mrs. Burroughs, who, supported by a couple of miners, was walking slowly away, having partly recovered.

With a roar as of a wild beast, McLaughlin threw down his knife. Divesting himself of his apron, he rushed from behind the block and made a pass at Power. The latter stepped quickly aside. As McLaughlin lurched heavily forward with the force of his own ineffective blow, Power floored him with a powerful stroke delivered full on the ruffian's face.

McLaughlin scrambled to his feet, but before he could put himself in position Power was upon him, raining blow after blow with smashing effect upon his antagonist's face and body until the latter sank insensible to the floor and stayed there, the bad blood and bad whiskey flowing from numerous wounds. Power then walked behind the block, selected a piece of meat, weighed it, calculated its value at 60 cents a pound and, placing the sum on the table, walked leisurely away.

"I think the man's dead, Power," called out a bystander.

"Well," said Power, "if he is dead you know where to find me." He walked to the hotel as cool and calm as if nothing unusual had occurred.

But Jem did not die. He did not belong to that class of whom it is said they die young because the gods love them. In the course of an hour or two he awoke from his drunken stupor. Although weak and groggy on his pins, as he himself expressed it, and bruised and battered about the face, and with both eyes nearly closed, he resumed his duties. Strange as it may appear, he emerged from the ordeal a changed man. From the hour that Power administered the drubbing a great reformation set in. Every trace of ruffianism had oozed out through his wounds. In place of the bully whom everyone feared and hated there stood a polite and decent man whose manners were all most obsequious and who never again was known to browbeat or insult a customer.

Women, children and dogs were the especial objects of his kind attentions. When he weighed a piece of meat he did not follow his former practice of weighing his heavy hand with it, but gave good measure, heaped up and running over. To Mrs. Burroughs he was more than kind, sending her the choicest bits and forgetting to charge them on the books. As for McDermott, he sent for him and told him that his dog would be fed daily if he would only let him come to the shop.

People who used to address him as "Mister" McLaughlin got to addressing him as McLaughlin, and finally they lapsed into the greater familiarity of "Mac" and "Jem." He received all these attentions with smiles of approval and happiness. The strangest part of the affair was that he never by any chance referred to the pounding he had received at the hands of Power. Asked as to how he received the injuries on the face he would attribute them to running against a side of beef in the dark. His memory of that event ever seemed a blank. All that he knew was that he had been hurt, he believed by accident, and that was all there was to be said. But the reformation was most marked. As long as I knew him afterwards he continued a steady and exemplary member of the community. He neither drank, gambled nor swore. "Boys," he remarked to one of his old companions, "I've drunk my last drink and I'm going to save my money from this time on forevermore till Kingdom come — so don't tempt me, for I won't go."

He was suspected of harboring matrimonial designs toward a Mrs. Weaver, who kept a restaurant on the flat, but as she had the inconvenient encumbrance of a husband still living, and told him so, the courtship came to naught. When Reverend Ebernezer Robson, the first Methodist missionary, paddled and poled his way in a canoe to Yale in 1859, McLaughlin gave him the glad hand. He also attended his first sermon on a Sunday morning and joined in singing the hymns. "You know," he explained, "I used to belong to a choir when I was a young fellow back in Maine."

There were sad days in store for Mrs. Burroughs in the tent down on the bar. She was destined to have a great heart trouble. Looking back as I write through all the years that have lapsed since then, I conjure up her frail figure as I last saw it, with her dear little ones close pressed to her breast and calling on God to protect and buoy them up in their great sorrow. That picture is one I never can forget.

One stormy afternoon a miner came into town. He had travelled rapidly over the trail from a bar where his company were located in quest of a surgeon. The story he told was that a stranger on his way down the river trail had shot himself in the thigh while climbing over a tree that had fallen across the path. The trigger caught on a twig and the charge exploded. A doctor was procured and accompanied the man back to Sailor Bar. When they reached there the stranger was dead — having bled to death. The doctor, after pronouncing the man to be dead, asked if he had any effects.

Some letters and a bag of gold dust weighing over $700 were handed to him. Every miner's cabin was provided with a pair of gold scales for weighing dust. From the purse the doctor weighed out $150 as his fee and handed the bag back to the miners. The latter brought the letters and the balance remaining in the bag to Yale, and handed them to the authorities. The letters were addressed "Charles Burroughs, Lytton," and bore the Yale postmark. Did anyone know such a person. Jem McLaughlin, who joined a group that had gathered to discuss the tragedy, suggested that Mrs. Burroughs might know the dead stranger.

"Gad!" exclaimed one of the group, "I'll bet any money that he's her husband."

"Go and ask her," suggested another.

"Not if I know myself," cried a third man. "I don't carry no bad news to no one, and could no more ask that poor thing if it's her husband than I could fly."

So it came about that in all that crowd of rough and uncouth men, who were accustomed to brave danger in every form, not one could be found with sufficient nerve to ask the little woman, "Was he your husband?"

The task was assigned to Mrs. Power and Mrs. Felker. The latter was the wife of Henry Felker of the Blue Tent. The surmise proved correct. The dead man was the woman's husband, who was on his way back to make her happy with his purse of gold when the accident occurred that took away his precious life.

A man who was on the trail with him when the gun went off told me that he was whistling and singing alternately as he walked along in anticipation of a reunion before nightfall with his loved ones, of whom he often spoke. "He was singing," said the man, "The Girl I Left Behind Me," and using his loaded gun as a staff, when the death-blow came."

Little more remains to be told. Mrs. Burroughs had the body brought to Yale and interred in the little cemetery. John Kurtz

The Fraser Canyon above Yale. Scores of miners drowned in its turbulent waters, were killed by Indians or, like the unfortunate Charles Burroughs, died in accidents.

read the funeral service, and Hugh Nelson, William Power, Jem McLaughlin and I led the pallbearers. At the grave the widow knelt, and with her children pressed to her bosom engaged in silent prayer, while we all drew back and gazed reverently at the affecting scene. When she rose, Jem McLaughlin respectfully and humbly came forward and took a child in each hand, while Power offered his arm to the afflicted woman. We then formed a little procession and marched down the hill to Mrs. Felker's where comfortable quarters had been prepared for the family. The following week they went away to their friends in California, and Yale knew them no more.

Was the regeneration of Jem McLaughlin permanent? I do not know. I hope that it was, for at the bottom he was a good sort and was capable of noble actions. Let us trust that he continued to grow in grace until when the end came he won a starry crown.

Sweet Marie

From 1861-65 over 600,000 soldiers died in the U.S. Civil War, with the author innocently involved and challenged to a duel.

Early in 1862 the United States Government appointed Allen Francis to be its Consul at Victoria. He was an urbane and kindly dispositioned man. His loyalty was unquestioned and, as this narrative will show, he was sufficiently skilled in the arts of diplomacy to successfully cope with the many clever minds that gathered at Victoria in that year with the avowed purpose of plotting against the government of their country and making this port the basis of operations for aiding the Southern rebels in their effort to destroy the Union. At the time of which I write, the bloody Civil War was raging between the Northern and the Southern States, and thousands of lives were daily lost in the struggle. The Northern armies had suffered many severe reverses, and the outcome of the war, which lasted through four long, weary years, was extremely doubtful.

In 1862 General Grant, whose skill was destined to save his country from disruption, was unborn as a great commander, and a rebel army had invaded the Northern State of Pennsylvania, leaving a train of death, desolation and misery in its track. The period was one of great anxiety for the friends of the Abraham Lincoln Government. As news of successive rebel victories was flashed over the wires, the friends of the South resident here became noisily jubilant and the friends of the Union correspondingly depressed.

Shortly after the outbreak of the war many sympathizers with the Slave States came to reside in Victoria. Some leased residences, others took apartments at hotels, still others went into business, while a fourth class proceeded to Cariboo and engaged in gold mining and trading.

Amongst the most prominent Southerners who went to Cariboo were Jerome and Thaddeus Harper and John and Oliver Jeffries. These men drove large bands of cattle from California and Oregon into Cariboo, and as beef was sold there at $1.50 a pound they realized large fortunes in a single season. The Harpers, who were from Virginia, took up land on the Mainland and became the cattle kings of the interior. (They founded the Gang Ranch, still the largest in B.C.) The two Jeffries, who were from the Slave State of Alabama, joined the Southern colony at Victoria. Having heaps of money, they were soon the leading spirits in an enterprise which, for audacity of conception, was unsurpassed by the most daring achievements of the Southerners during the whole of that awful contest.

The Mathieson brothers, two German caterers, built a new brick hotel, naming it the St. Nicholas, on Government Street, across the road from the New England. They opened it early in the fall of 1862, and did a roaring business. I took a room on the second floor and ate my meals at the Hotel de France. The Jeffries engaged apartments on the upper floor of the St. Nicholas, and fitted them up handsomely. They entertained their Southern and Victoria friends liberally. A Mr. and Mrs. Pusey, also Southerners, had a room on the second floor just opposite mine.

At Ringo's Hotel on Yates Street resided a handsome young American, claiming to be a Southerner, named Richard Lovell. He was a great favorite of the Jeffries as, indeed, he was of everyone who came in contact with him. He dressed well and his only fault was a habit of sprinkling his handkerchiefs and garments with a powerful and pungent perfume. Now, it happens that I have a natural repugnance for perfumery, and I apprised Lovell of that fact when we had become well acquainted. He laughed and said that it was a habit into which he had fallen and could not break off. "Besides," he added, "it keeps down the smell of tobacco after I have smoked."

"Of the two," I rejoined, "I prefer the weed. In fact, I'd prefer a whiff of sewer-gas any day to the odor of perfumery."

"Every man to his taste or smell," rejoined Dick good-naturedly, and the conversation ended. He little thought, nor did I, that his fondness for scent would prove his undoing.

The St. Nicholas Hotel has passed through many phases and hands since the Mathieson brothers failed and died. It is now known as the Savoy, and in company with Mr. Stevenson, the present proprietor, I not long since ascended the upper floor and entered rooms No. 23 and 24 for the first time in forty-one years. Except in the furnishings, few changes have been made in that long interval. But ah! if those walls could speak what tales they would narrate of the scenes that have transpired within their four corners since I last sat and talked and smoked and drank toasts and sang therein!

Mr. Pusey was a slim, gray man of about fifty. His wife was a large and forceful personage, stout and large-limbed. She had a passion for loading her pretty fingers — for she had small, lovely hands — with costly diamonds, and her earrings, if genuine stones, were worth much. Mr. Pusey's face wore a tired, shrinking look — a sort of excuse-me-for-being-alive expression; his wife, on the other hand, was self-assertive. She was emotional and intensely Southern in her ideas, and claimed that a white man had as much right to buy and sell niggers as he had to buy and sell cattle or merchandise. I did not agree with her, but I thought it unwise to say so. I simply acquiesced and let the idea that I was a Southern sympathizer take hold of the lady's mind and remain there undisturbed. So we became good friends.

The Jeffries and Puseys often gave little "evenings," to which Dick Lovell and I and many others were invited. Mrs. Pusey could sing a little, and one night she brought with her to the Jeffries' room a young lady whom she introduced as "Miss Jackson, a niece of Stonewall Jackson, the famous Southern general." Miss Jackson was about thirty years of age and rather nice looking, but she did not strike me as being at all girlish in her figure or ways. As a matter of fact, I addressed her as "Mrs." Jackson until corrected by Mrs. Pusey. Miss Jackson had a guitar and Oliver Jeffries could blow through the hole of a flute and make a loud noise, which, in his conceit, he thought was music.

All the gentlemen could join in the choruses, and cigars having been passed round and a decanter of dark brandy and another of Hudson's Bay rum having gone the rounds "with the sun," and the ladies having had their share, the singing of patriotic songs was commenced. The notes of "Way Down South in Dixie" and "My Maryland" floated out into the night air or filled the corridors with uncertain harmony, but the evenings were jolly and all were extremely happy.

On one occasion we became exceedingly boisterous. News had come of a great rebel victory, and the company excelled all previous efforts in singing Confederate airs. The two rooms were crowded and the rejoicing was kept up until early morning. Lovell was especially enthusiastic. He excelled all others present in the exuberance of his language and the extravagance of his actions. The ladies were delighted with Dick, and when he staggered away for his hotel he was voted a jolly good fellow and an uncompromising rebel. When, later on, I left rooms 23 and 24 John Jeffries insisted upon accompanying me.

As I unlocked my door he entered, uninvited, and, turning

the key on the inside, put it in his pocket. I made a mental note that it was a rather cheeky proceeding to make a man a prisoner in his own room, but I said nothing and calmly awaited results. Jeffries examined the window; it was secure. He looked at the transom; it was closed. He tried the door; it was fast. He looked beneath the bed; no one was there. He opened the wardrobe and felt among the clothes. Then he turned sharply around and regarded me closely for a full minute. I did not enjoy the scrutiny and said so; moreover, I told him curtly that I wished to go to bed, Then he spoke:

"Higgins," he began, "pardon me, but I have something to

During the U.S. Civil War between the North and the South there were many sympathizers from both sides in Victoria. With his huge Stars and Stripes, the owner of the city's California Saloon proclaimed to all that he favored the North.

say to you of vast importance. It is a close secret, known only to George Coe, bookkeeper at Goldstone & Co.'s, Jerome Harper, Dick Lovell, Mrs. Pusey, Oliver and myself. We want your help and have decided to take you into the scheme. Should you decline you must take an oath never to repeat what I am about to tell you."

I told him I had decided objection to making a promise before I knew what was required of me.

He begged hard, and I finally gave the pledge. He then said: "We intend to fit out a privateer at Victoria to prey on American shipping. A treasure ship leaves San Francisco twice a month with from $2 to 3 million in gold dust for the East. With a good boat we can intercept and rob and burn two of those steamers on the lonely Mexican coast and return to Victoria with $5 million dollars before the Washington Government will have heard of the incident."

"But," I urged, "you'll be caught and handed over to the American authorities for piracy, and then you'll be hanged."

"Not at all. Look at the privateers *Alabama* and *Shenandoah*. They have destroyed millions of dollars' worth of American shipping and they sail in and out of French and British ports unmolested. They hold letters of marque from the Confederate Government, and England and France have recognized the Southern States as belligerents."

"But," I said, "without letters of marque you will be pirates all the same."

"Well," he replied, "I have them in my room, signed by Jeff Davis and sealed by Judah P. Benjamin, Secretary of State. We have officers here and a strong crew. All we want is a suitable vessel. The *Otter*, and the more ancient *Beaver*, of the Hudson's Bay Company, can be bought, but they are not suitable — too slow and frail. We have got our eyes at last on a good ship and can get her for the business. But we require outside help and we have selected you to do a certain thing for us."

"What do you want me to do?" I asked.

"You know the Consul well. He is clever, but a man in whom he has confidence can fool him. You and he are close friends. An article will be prepared by Coe for your paper which will mislead him and put him and his detectives on the wrong scent. While they are following that scent we shall get away in our ship, and without railroads or telegraphs anywhere on the coast, and with no warship convenient to follow, we shall be back with the treasure in six weeks."

I confess that while this bold man, who believed implicitly in the justice of his cause and purpose, spoke I felt a creepy feeling come over me. I wished he had kept his secret. I had no intention of doing as he wished, but I was afraid, actually afraid, to tell him so. He looked so earnest and fiendish and I had reason to think he carried a knife and revolver ready for use, while I was unarmed. He awaited my answer and I asked for time — a couple of days. After pressing very hard for an immediate decision, he consented to give the time, adding significantly that he thought I had better agree. He then unlocked the door and bade me good night. I watched him until he disappeared and then I became sensible of a strong odor that filled the passage.

"If I did not know that Dick Lovell has been abed for the last hour I'd be ready to swear that he's not far from this room now. Ugh! that awful smell. I'd detect it anywhere. If that man should commit a crime he could be traced from Victoria to Halifax by his scent." Thus soliloquizing, I locked my door and fell asleep.

In the morning HMS *Clio*, Captain Turnour commanding, dropped anchor in Esquimalt harbour. She had come from Honolulu. Among her midshipmen was Lord Charles Beresford, one of the bravest of the many brave sailors in our service. The *Clio* brought the information that Lord Charles, while ashore at Honolulu, had torn the American coat-of-arms from its position over the entrance to the Consulate, taken it aboard the *Clio* and hung it up in his cabin as a trophy. The published account proceeded to say that Captain Turnour, when informed of the outrage, manned a launch and conducted the young midshipman to the Consulate, where, after offering a humble apology to the Consul and the United States Government, Lord Charles ascended a ladder and restored the emblem to its former position.

The news of the insult to the United States Government at Honolulu gave the greatest satisfaction to the secessionist colony at Victoria. Then some graceless rebels went at night to the Consulate, and painted a "plug" hat on the head and a pipe in the mouth of the eagle that forms the central figure of the American arms. A liberal award was offered, but the perpetrators were never discovered. The following day two English bootblacks were paid $10 to allow a small Confederate flag to be raised over their establishment.

The Unionists were indignant and appealed to the police, who, of course, could do nothing. They therefore proceeded in a body to tear down the offensive emblem, but twenty or thirty determined-looking men formed a solid phalanx in front of the shop and the flag waved till noon, when it was voluntarily lowered. Mrs. Pusey was on springs during all this excitement. Her husband, who had not the least control over her, was always referred to contemptuously as "Mrs. Pusey's husband."

While these things were happening, the time when I must decide to accept or reject Jeffries' proposition was drawing near. I was extremely nervous. I blamed myself for having had anything to do in a social way with a body of men and women with whose principles and ideas I had no sympathy. I saw that my duplicity in making them think that I approved of the Confederate cause, merely for the sake of having "a good time," was about to bring upon me a righteous punishment. Happen what might, I was determined not to deceive the Consul. He was a warm personal friend, and I was always a welcome visitor at his home. He had trusted me and told me some things in confidence which I could not reveal. Jeffries had done the same, and altogether I was in a pretty fix. Finally, I hit upon a plan which I hoped would bring me out of my difficulty.

I decided to keep away from the conspirators, to tell no one of the proposition, and return no answer to Jeffries if I could help it. I left the St. Nicholas and engaged a room at the Hotel de France.

About two hours after the time set for my answer had expired I was walking along Government Street, when Oliver Jeffries tapped me on the shoulder and said: "John is awaiting your answer."

"Tell him I've no answer to give him," I replied.

"You promised."

"Yes, but I've changed my mind. I'll have nothing to do with the plot, but I won't betray him."

Oliver regarded me with a ferocious glare and then turned and walked abruptly away. Towards evening George Cox entered my office and handed me a note. It was a challenge to fight John Jeffries. He proposed that we should go to San Juan Island, then in joint occupation of the American and British Governments, both maintaining a small garrison there, and engage in a duel.

I must have turned as pale as death, but I managed to say that I would consult a friend, and the gentleman went away. It took me fully half an hour to pull myself together. Then I walked over to the Hotel de France, not that I had any appetite, but I wanted time to think the matter over. I took a seat at one of the tables and buried my face in my hands, cursing myself for all sorts of a fool for having got into such a mess.

As I sat there a cheery voice exclaimed: "Halloa, what's the matter with you? Are you ill?"

I looked up and saw standing at the table Augustine Hibbard, a native of Montreal, but who had become an American citizen, with whom I was on most intimate terms and whose company I much enjoyed.

He sat down and I told him that I had been challenged to fight a duel by an American rebel. Now Hibbard, who was a strong friend of the Union, was as brave as a lion, and seemed to enjoy my confusion.

"Accept the challenge and I'll be your second," he cried.

"Hibbard," I pleaded. "I just can't fight. I've turned over a new leaf. I intend to lead another and better life. To tell you the truth, last night I proposed to one of the sweetest and loveliest of her sex and was accepted. It is too bad, just when I have the sum of human happiness within my grasp to have to drop all and fight a duel about nothing! No, I won't meet him. She would never speak to me again, even if I should escape with my life, which isn't likely."

"By heavens," cried Hibbard, "you shall either fight or I'll fight for you. I'll go and see these men — wait here till I return." He started for the St. Nicholas on a half run.

He was back in half an hour and reported that he had seen both Jeffries and Coe and told them I was eager for the fray; that I was a dead shot with a revolver and he had chosen that weapon; that I had fought and winged my man in Texas (a place I was never in).

"Hibbard," I groaned, "you know all this is untrue."

"My dear lad," he cut in, "I am a second. A second is a diplomat. A diplomat is an official liar. Ergo, I am an unofficial liar."

I smiled and he rattled on, saying that if he hadn't scared my opponents he had at least made them believe that I was a most dangerous ruffian who was thirsting for Jeffries' blood. "I've set them thinking," he added. As we conversed, Mr. and Mrs. Pusey entered the hotel, having seen us seated there. They were much excited. Mrs. Pusey was hysterical, speaking loudly, laughing and crying alternately.

"What do you think?" she began, "I have just ascertained that my room has been entered, my drawers searched and valuable papers stolen. There was money there, but the thieves did not touch it, and, strange to say, there was the strongest odor of perfume in the room when I first entered. I cannot account for it, for I never use perfumery. The room smelt just like Lovell, who has never been in the room, to my knowledge."

After expressing my regret I left the Puseys and Hibbard and walked down to the Consulate to consult with Mr. Francis. He retired with me into a little den back of the main office. As he closed the door I detected a strong smell of Lovell's peculiar perfume. I sniffed and said: "That smells like Dick Lovell."

"Lovell? Lovell?" asked the old gentleman. "Who is he?"

"Oh!" I replied, "he is a rebel friend of mine."

I then told him that I had been challenged because I had expressed hostility to the Confederacy. I uttered not a word as to the true reason. He expressed sympathy, promised secrecy, and I went away. I passed several anxious hours thinking over the affair in which I was to engage as a principal. Four years before I had seen the body of Sloane, an unfortunate youth who was shot on Church Hill in a duel, and a vision of that dreadful scene haunted me as I walked on. [See page 79.]

What if I should share the same fate? What if I should escape with my life, but lose my right hand, as my friend Racey Biven did, in a duel with Jimmy Dorsey at Oakland, California, in 1855? How could I earn my bread with only the left hand? Suppose I lost a leg, or my lungs were perforated and I lived on for years a public burthen? Better be dead than a cripple or a hopeless invalid.

A little white dog bounded and leaped on the sidewalk and barked a joyous welcome as I entered the master's shop. I imagined that the people I met on the street regarded me with deep interest, as though they knew all about it and were looking at a man who was either going to commit a murder or had received a death sentence.

When I got inside the shop a lady at the counter seemed to stare at me with an expression of keen interest on her face, and a little girl put her hand in mine and said: "You look 'ick." I bought some trifling articles, and as I hurried from the shop I ran against Willis Bond, who had once been a slave, and now was a house-mover, an orator and a politician. He was one of the cleverest men, white or black, that I have ever met.

"Say, boss," said Bond, "Youse looks pale. Is you sick?"

"No," I replied, "I am quite well."

"Well," persisted Bond, after a long stare, "I'd like to be white, but I don't want to look so much like Mr. Hamblet's father's ghost as you does."

I went to my office and tried to write, but no use; I could not form a sentence. I went outside again and met Dick Lovell — the man was as debonaire as ever and bitter in his denunciation of the United States Government. Evidently he had not heard of my quarrel with Jeffries, or if he had he chose to ignore it. I was in no mood for talking. I met Hibbard by appointment at the Hotel de France.

He informed me, much to my disappointment and disgust, that the duel would come off on San Juan Island near his lime kiln, and that he had suggested a glade close to his house for the contest. Boats would be ready the next morning to take us across. I suppose there was never a more miserable man in the world than I was at that moment. I was utterly prostrated, not so much from a feeling of fear (although I was really scared), as from a knowledge that I was about to die a thoroughly innocent man. As we conversed, Oliver Jeffries entered the hotel bar and, walking rapidly towards me, reached out his hand. I think I grasped it convulsively, for I had a feeling that there was to be a reconciliation. I know that I felt a great lump rise in my throat.

"Higgins," he exclaimed, and his eyes shone with a kindly light, "we've done you a great wrong. We've caught the traitor, and you're absolved."

"What do you mean?" I asked, eagerly.

"An hour ago, while John and I were breakfasting, our room was entered and a tin box stolen. It contained papers of great value. As in the Puseys' case, no money was taken, but the room smelt just like Lovell. So we went at once to Ringo's and bounded up the stairs. The door was locked. John kicked it in and there stood Lovell with our box in his hand, open, and the papers scattered on the bed. I seized the papers and John knocked the sweet-scented ... down and nearly kicked the life out of him. We left him lying on the floor and John sent me here to apologize for his mean opinion of you."

I was nearly beside myself with joy. The flowing bowl was filled and emptied and refilled and emptied again before the young rebel was allowed to depart with a blessing and a kind message for his brother. Hibbard was greatly disappointed; he said he would have enjoyed seeing a rebel shot or shooting one himself.

I reminded him of the letter a British officer wrote home from India, in which he said it is "rare fun when you hunt a tiger, but when a tiger hunts you....!"

The evening of the day on which the duel had been declared off and Lovell exposed as a spy, the United States steamer *Shubrick*, a well-armed and manned vessel, arrived from across the Sound and was brought alongside the Hudson's Bay Company's wharf. On board was Mr. Victor Smith, collector of customs for Puget Sound District. He was a personal friend of President Abraham Lincoln, and an unswerving loyalist. Immediately after tying the *Shubrick* to the wharf, Mr. Smith proceeded to discharge all the crew and officers except Captain Selden, the commander, and Mr. Winship, the chief engineer. All except these two officers were more than suspected of disloyalty and of an intention to seize the ship, convert her into a privateer, and capture the San Francisco steamers referred to by Jeffries in his conversation with me. Lovell, who was in the secret, had kept Mr. Francis and Smith informed of the plot. "Miss Jackson" was also a spy in the pay of the Consul. In a day or two a fresh crew joined the *Shubrick*, and the conspirators went out of business.

A few days later I called on Consul Francis and proceeded to tell my story. The kind old gentleman laid his hand on my shoulder and said: "I know all that you are about to say. I knew what was going on all the time. My detectives kept me well informed. I knew how sorely you were tempted to do me an injury, and how you refused, and I was determined that not a hair of your head should be hurt. Had the party reached San Juan Island, your antagonist and his friends would have been taken to the guardhouse by our soldiers there. Lovell is a grand detective. He overheard Jeffries tempting you in your room that night, and did all his work well."

"But," I said, "the windows and transom were tightly closed by Jeffries."

"Yes," interposed the Consul, "but he forgot the keyhole. Lovell has phenomenal hearing and can see in the dark!"

"Ah!" I said, "I scented him when I went into the hall."

"Hibbard also told me about the duel, and his part in the plot was to induce the gang to go to San Juan Island and so get them into the hands of the American garrison," said the Consul.

Mr. Francis was a man with a soul and a heart and as he spoke his voice quivered with emotion, and something like a tear glistened in his eye. "Thank God." he concluded, "the long strain is over. The rebel camp at Victoria is broken up and dispersed at last. Victor Smith and I can now take a much-needed rest."

Nearly all the chief actors in the stirring scenes I have narrated are dead, and strange to relate, with one or two exceptions, all died from violence. Victor Smith perished in the wreck of the steamship *Brother Jonathan* in 1865. Consul Francis was killed by a fire engine at St. Thomas, Ontario; Augustine Hibbard was shot by his partner at the San Juan Island lime kiln in 1869; Oliver Jeffries dropped dead at Portland, Oregon; and George Coe died of consumption in Idaho. John Jeffries was killed in a run-away accident at Walla Walla. Jerome Harper went mad and drowned himself in a bathtub at San Jose, California, and his partner, Thaddeus Harper, after suffering for several years from the effects of a kick by a horse on the head, died at Victoria's Jubilee Hospital. Dick Lovell went back East and accompanied the Union Army to the battlefield of Gettysburg, and was killed there.

But, the reader will say, you headed the story "Sweet Marie." Who and what was she? You have not mentioned her once in the whole reminiscence. To which I reply that she trickles like a fragrant essence through the whole story. "Sweet Marie" was the brand of powerful perfume that Dick Lovell used on his handkerchiefs and clothing.

B.C.'s Worst Marine Disaster

**The *Pacific* should never have left
the scrapyard, but crowded aboard were
some 500 passengers.**

This unhappy tale revives recollections which, were I to consult
my own private feelings, I would gladly allow to remain undisturbed in the misty records of the past. But he who takes the role
of faithful chronicler of historical events should not shrink from
the performance of a task, however distasteful or painful it may
be to him or to those whose reputations may suffer by the
narration. Sentiment should not be allowed to interfere with the
duty of the historian, even though dead and buried animosities
be called back to life and old wounds opened and made to bleed
afresh.

I propose to tell the story of the terrible loss of the steamship
Pacific which occurred in 1875. I think I can fairly claim that, with
the exception of the two people out of hundreds who survived
the wreck, there is no person now living who is in a position to
give as correct a narrative of that awful tragedy and the circumstances that led to it as me. There has never been a doubt in my
mind that those circumstances were preventable — that had the
crudest precautions been adopted and the commonest decencies
of life observed, the disaster would never have taken place.

The steamship *Pacific* was built in New York in 1851. She was
less than 900 tons burthen, and fifty years ago was considered a
"crack" vessel, fitted with all the (then) modern improvements.
Today it is safe to say that no vessel of her class would receive a
permit to put to sea with passengers. She might be tolerated as
a freighter, but it is doubtful if a crew would be found to man
her.

If such was her condition when the *Pacific* first took the
water, what must have been her state when, twenty-five years

Opposite: The *Pacific*, resurrected from the ships' boneyard with catastrophic consequences.

Captain Jefferson D. Howell, right, delayed the *Pacific's* sailing because he had a headache.

Charles Seymour, captain of the *Orpheus* which holed the *Pacific*. He did not stop to aid the sinking vessel.

later, under the command of Captain Jefferson D. Howell, she left Victoria harbour on her last voyage. She was loaded to the gunwale with freight and so filled with passengers that all the berth room was occupied and the saloons and decks were utilized as sleeping spaces. I do not believe that anyone, not even the agents or officers of the steamer, knew the exact number of persons she carried on that fateful voyage. There was a brisk competition between the Goodall & Perkins line, to which the *Pacific* belonged, and the Pacific Mail Steamship Company which had shortly before secured a lucrative contract for carrying the mails between Victoria and San Francisco. Fare on the *Pacific* was reduced to $5, and if a party of three or four applied for tickets they were taken at $2.50 a head.

On the morning of November 4, 1875, having business with a gentleman named Conway, one of the passengers, I was on the wharf before the hour at which the steamer was advertised to sail —nine a.m. I found the boat so crowded that the crew could scarcely move about the decks. I have always contended that the passengers numbered at least 500.

This belief has been disputed; but it has never been successfully disputed. The agents' list showed that only 270 passengers were booked at Victoria. But there was a large list from Puget Sound, and it was admitted that scores took passage without having secured tickets, competition being so keen that some were carried for nothing to keep them from patronizing the opposing line. Besides, small children paid no fares, and were not counted.

The morning was dark and lowering. Heavy clouds moved slowly overhead. A fall of rain had preceded the coming of the sun, but there were no signs that indicated worse weather than is usual in this latitude in the fall of the year. I think I must have known at least one hundred of the persons who took passage that day, and who, twelve hours later, found a watery grave in Juan de Fuca Strait.

Captain and Mrs. Otis Parsons and child, with Mrs. Thorne, a sister of Mrs. Parsons, were amongst those to whom I said farewell and wished bon voyage. The captain had sold his interest in Fraser River steamers and was on his way to California.

Having said goodbye to Parsons and his family, I reached with difficulty a spot where Miss Fannie Palmer, youngest daughter of Professor Digby Palmer, stood. This young lady was a bright and lovely member of Victoria society. She was most popular, and naturally attracted a large circle of admirers. Her fond mother was in the group that surrounded the fair girl, whose sweet face was more than usually animated in anticipation of the round of pleasure that awaited her upon arrival at the popular city of San Francisco a few days hence. There were other fair and joyous maidens on board, and there were young mothers in the first bloom of womanhood, with children at their sides or in their arms. There were matrons whose grownup children had come to the wharf to see them safely off, and bless their departure and pray for their preservation, for no one felt any confidence in the old steamer. Every class, every nationality, every age were assembled on the deck of that doomed vessel. The last hands I grasped were those of S.P. Moody, of the Moodyville Sawmill Company and Frank Garesche, private banker and Wells, Fargo & Company agent. As I descended the gang plank, I met a lady with a little boy in her arms. The way was steep, and I volunteered to carry the little fellow aboard. He was handed to me, and I toiled up the plank and delivered him to his mother. The wee, blue-eyed boy put up his lips to be kissed, and waved his little hands as I turned to go. Then mother and child were swallowed up in the dense throng, and I saw them no more forever!

The ship, as I have said, was billed to sail at nine o'clock. She did not get off until nearly an hour later. The same thing happened at Tacoma the day previous. The steamer was advertised to leave at noon. She did not leave until evening. The captain, who was in bed, had given orders that he should not be disturbed until he awoke. So a mail-carrying vessel, with steam up and a big crowd of passengers anxious to get on, was detained because the commander had a headache and must not be disturbed! It was nearly ten o'clock when Captain Howell appeared on the bridge at Victoria and the order was given to cast off.

Had that order been given at nine o'clock, in all human probability the ship would have escaped the peril which awaited her, and this dismal chapter would never have been written. Some people will persist in attributing disaster and sickness and ill-fortune to the Divine will, but if the whole world were to cry out that the *Pacific* was lost because God willed it, I should say that the vessel went down because the most ordinary precautions for safety were violated by her officers. I do not think that the captain realized the importance and gravity of the duties he had undertaken to discharge. I do not believe he ever reflected that in his hands were placed the lives and property of several hundreds of his fellow beings and that upon his judgment, sobriety and care depended their safety.

The *Pacific* was a bad ship and an unlucky one. She had been sunk once before, and for two years previous to the breaking out of the Cassiar gold fever in Northwestern B.C. had been laid away in the Company's "boneyard" at San Francisco. She was taken and fitted up to accommodate the rush of people to the new gold fields. She was innately rotten, but the paint and putty thickly daubed on covered much of the rottenness, as paint and powder hide the wrinkles and crow's feet of a society belle. Scarcely anyone was aware of the ship's real condition, although she was regarded as unsafe.

As the vessel swung off, the multitude on the wharf gave three rousing cheers to speed departing friends on their way. The response was loud and hearty. Hands and handkerchiefs were waved and last messages exchanged until the vessel had disappeared around the first point. A belated Englishman, who had passed the previous night in a wild revel, and who had taken a ticket by the *Pacific*, was the "last man" on this occasion. As the vessel passed out, the belated one appeared on the wharf with his hand-bag and a steamer trunk. He shouted and signalled, but all to no purpose.

The boat kept on her way, and the man danced up and down in his rage. Then he sat down on his trunk and cursed the boat and all its belongings. If the man read the papers five days later he must have thanked his stars that the captain did not put back to take him on board, and no doubt he recalled all his naughty words.

It was Thursday when the steamer sailed. On Friday, Saturday and Sunday heavy storms prevailed, and the telegraph lines went down. Until Monday afternoon there was no communication by wire with the outer world. About noon on the afternoon of the 8th of November, Mr. W.F. Archibald, who was the chief operator of Victoria, received this message from Port Townsend:

A ship has arrived here with a man named Jelly aboard, who was picked up Saturday floating on a piece of wreckage off the entrance to the Straits. He says the steamship Pacific *sank last Thursday night, and he fears that all on board were lost but himself.*

Then the wires again went down, and no further information could be obtained through that medium. An hour or two later the steamer *North Pacific* came in from Puget Sound. On board was Henry F. Jelly, the rescued passenger. The whole town rushed to the wharf. I was fortunate in interviewing the man. From him, I learned that the *Pacific* ran into a sailing ship while off Cape Flattery, about ten o'clock on the night of the day on which she sailed from Victoria, and sank in ten minutes.

The greatest consternation prevailed. The officers lost their presence of mind (if they ever had any), and the crew were too intent in endeavoring to ensure their own safety to pay attention to the passengers, who ran wildly about the deck and through the saloons. In the crush Mrs. Parsons' child was torn from her arms and killed, and the last that Jelly saw of the bereaved mother was when she stepped into one of the boats still pressing her dead child to her breast. This boat was swamped in lowering, and all who had entrusted themselves to it were lost at the side of the fast sinking ship.

Some of the life (death?) boats were found to have been filled with water to steady the ship. Before the water could be run off, the passengers and the crew crowded in and would not get out. So all attempts to lower the boats had to be abandoned. There were a number of Chinese on board. They were among the first to get into the boats, and laid themselves down on the bottom. They were pulled out and thrown screaming into the sea to make room for white passengers.

There was no order, no discipline, no one to give directions. It was every man for himself. All seemed to have gone stark mad in the face of the great danger that beset them. A rush was made for life-preservers. The number available was not sufficient.

All this time the vessel was sinking, her rail almost even with the water, when several of the male passengers leaped overboard and drowned themselves. Others shut themselves in their cabins and awaited the grim messenger calmly. There were several trained horses on board, the property of the Rockwell & Hurlburt troupe. These animals had been exhibited at Victoria the day before the vessel sailed. They were gifted with rare intelligence. One, a large white gelding, was almost human in his knowledge. This horse was found floating in the Straits saddled and bridled some days after the wreck. It was thought one of the troupe mounted him in the vain hope of being carried ashore on his back.

The screaming and shouting of the men and women as they rushed back and forth wringing their hands and jostling and trampling down one another in their frenzy must have been terrible to hear and see. Absolutely, beyond the lowering of the one boat that was swamped at the side, nothing was done to save a single life. All was confusion and despair. The officers might as well have been ashore for all the good they did on board. As the supreme moment approached some of the unfortunate clasped hands, others sank on their knees and offered up hurried prayers.

A lady passenger tore the diamonds from her ears and put them with a purse of gold into a sailor's hands, imploring him to take them and save her life. Several families gathered together and with tears and lamentations awaited the end. The people in the boats made vain efforts to swing them from the davits, in their excitement forgetting that while they remained in the boats they could not be lifted from the deck. In that spirit of selfishness which seizes upon most men in the face of extreme peril, no one would give up his place for fear some one else would occupy it.

So they remained helplessly huddled together while Death came on with ever-shortening steps. Presently the ship lurched, and every beam seemed to crack.

A cry of despair ascended from the doomed company as the decks opened before the combined pressure of air and water with a great roar, as though a thousand boilers had burst simultaneously. The next moment the *Pacific* sank beneath the troubled waves and the sea was dotted with wreckage and drowning men and women, whose cries were pitiful to hear. Jelly, with three others, managed to secure a hencoop, and floated away with the tide. In a few minutes the last solitary shriek, the bubbling cry, died away.

Jelly and his companions so far as they knew, were alone on that wild waste of water. The night was intensely dark and the waves frequently broke over the wreckage on which the poor men were. Before daylight two had been washed away. When the sun came up the third man went out of his mind, and before evening leaped into the sea and disappeared. Two days after the disaster Jelly was picked up by a passing vessel and taken to Port Townsend. From that port a revenue cutter was despatched to the scene of the wreck.

On the way out of the Straits, Neil Henley, a quartermaster of the wrecked vessel, was found floating on a piece of wreckage and saved. He reported that Captain Howell, the second mate, the cook and four passengers (one a young lady) were on the wreckage with him when the ship first went down. All perished one by one until only he remained. The young lady, from the description, was believed to be a Miss Reynolds, of San Francisco, who was returning home from a visit to friends at Esquimalt. Once she was washed off the raft, and the second mate plunged in and rescued her. She resumed her place on the raft, but seemed to lose all hope. Gradually her strength departed and she lay motionless on the fragment until a wave washed her away, her heroic rescuer soon following.

From Victoria a steamer was despatched to the vicinity of Cape Flattery. She returned in a few days with four bodies — three men and a woman. The men were identified. One was a merchant from Puyallup, and two were members of the *Pacific's* crew. The rescue of Henley cleared away much of the mist that had obscured Jelly's statement.

Henley was asleep in the forecastle when the crash came. He said the water flowed in at the bows of the steamer with a rush. He was awake and on deck in an instant and saw a large ship off the starboard bow. This vessel afterwards proved to be the American ship *Orpheus*, bound for Puget Sound. She was commanded by C.A. Sawyer, who made no effort to assist the *Pacific*, but stood off for Vancouver Island, and a day or two later his vessel was hopelessly wrecked in Barclay Sound.

His excuse for his inaction was that he believed his own vessel to be sinking. He explained that he stood across the *Pacific's* bow — and so caused the collision — for the purpose of speaking to her and learning his whereabouts. He always claimed that had there been a proper lookout on the steamer there would have been no disaster. HMS *Repulse* passed out of the Straits on the night of the wreck, and it was said by some of the sailors that they reported to the captain that blue lights were burning on the port side, but that no attention was paid to the report.

The woman whose body was brought in was a tourist who was returning to San Francisco. About ten days after the disaster the body of Miss Palmer was brought from San Juan Island and buried during a heavy fall of snow. In spite of the storm the cortege was one of the largest ever seen in Victoria, so great was the sympathy felt for the father and mother of the bright young spirit whose light had been so untimely quenched.

As the days wore on other bodies came ashore and were either brought to Victoria or interred where found. At Beacon Hill, ten days after the wreck, I saw the body of Mr. Conway, whom I had gone to the wharf to see on the morning the steamer sailed, rolling in the surf. The body was easily recognized. When the ship sailed he had a large sum of money in his possession, but when he was picked up everything of value was gone.

One day some Beechy Bay Indians arrived in the harbour in a canoe towing another canoe in which was the body of a large man. The body was recognized as the remains of J.H. Sullivan, the Cassiar Gold Commissioner, who had sailed with hopes of being with his friends in Ireland, and spending the Christmas holidays with them. In his pockets were a considerable sum in drafts and gold, a gold watch and chain, and a pocket diary. In the diary, evidently written just before the unfortunate gentleman had retired to his cabin, was this entry:

Left Victoria for old Ireland on Thursday, 4th, about noon. Passed Cape Flattery about 4 p.m. Some of the miners drunk; some ladies sick; feel sorry at temporarily leaving a country in which I have lived so long; spent last evening at dear old Hillside.

About a month after the ship had gone down, and when the first burst of grief had been replaced by a feeling of resignation, and while the shores were still patrolled for many miles in the hope of finding more bodies, a man walking along the southern face of Beacon Hill observed a fragment of wreckage lying high and dry on the beach. Upon examination it proved to be part of a stateroom stanchion or support.

The only survivors of the 375 to 500 people on board were F.H. Jelly, top left, and Neil Henley, top right.

Among the victims were Provincial Police Superintendent J.H. Sullivan, above left, who had supervised the hanging of Tom Chooley (see page 184), and S.P. Moody, above right. The board on which Moody wrote his last message is today on display at the Vancouver Maritime Museum.

On its white surface were written in a bold business hand, with a pencil, these words:

S.P. MOODY. ALL LOST.

The handwriting was identified as that of S.P. Moody, the principal owner of the Moodyville Sawmills. It is supposed that when he found the ship going down and no hope remained of saving his life, Mr. Moody wrote this "message from the sea" on the stanchion in the faint hope that it might some day be picked up, and his fate known. This hope was not in vain. I believe the piece of wreckage with the inscription upon it is still cherished by the Moody family.

As I gazed at Conway's body, I remembered another incident that befell me just after the *Pacific* left Victoria. I was walking home and encountered Mrs. Digby Palmer. She was gazing with glistening eyes towards the outer harbour, where there was quite a grove of tall forest trees. Above the tops of these trees the smoke of the departing steamer was rising in great black billows and losing itself in space. It was this smoke Mrs. Palmer was watching. As I approached she exclaimed: "I'm seeing the last of Fannie!" Alas! how true it was. The poor mother's fond eyes had seen the last of her dear child. The body of that child, after being the sport of the cruel waves for ten days, was borne in the arms of the tide past her Victoria home and laid on the beach at San Juan Island, almost within sight of the house she had left a short time before so full of life and girlish glee and happiness.

Inquests held upon the bodies that were found placed the blame on the *Orpheus* for crossing the steamer's bows and causing the collision. The inefficiency of the watch on the steamer was condemned, and the condition of the boats was denounced, but nothing ever came of the verdict. The owners of the boats were never prosecuted, and the officers were all dead. The families who were bereft of their bread-winners were not compensated for their loss.

I have often narrated the dreadful story of the loss of the *Pacific* to friends who had heard only a vague account of it. On several occasions, as I concluded the narrative, I have been asked which incident of the many pathetic ones connected with the wreck dwelt most in my mind. In other words, which of the occurrences impressed me most.

I have always replied that the one picture which presents itself to my mind when I recall the awful event is that of the bonnie little blue-eyed boy to whom I said farewell as the gang plank was drawn in. I had never seen him before — he was neither kith nor kin of mine — but whenever I think of the going down of the *Pacific* his sweet face appears before me. Sometimes, as I last saw it, full of beauty, confidence, and mirth; at other times wearing an expression of keen anguish and horror, the bright eyes filled with tears and the hands held out in a vain petition to be saved from an impending doom.

Since I sat down to write this sad story he has been with me every moment of the time; and once I thought I heard him repeat what I have often in the silent hours of the day or night imagined I heard him say: "You placed me in this coffin; cannot you help me out?"

Alas! If I had but known.

The Passing of a Race

Home-made whiskey sold by predatory whites protected by dishonest policemen transformed proud Indian tribes into rag-clad remnants.

"How many lives do you think the Indian whiskey manufacturers at Victoria destroyed, directly or indirectly, by their traffic?" I was asked one day in the early 1900s. I replied that the number would be difficult to estimate. But when I say that the western and southern shores of the harbour were once populated by some 4,000 members of the northern tribes but now only by about ninety, some idea of the terrible inroads that were made upon the tribes may be conceived.

A rough census taken in 1859 gave a native population in and about Victoria of 8,500. In July 1858, the Songish tribe were visited by the Mackah tribe, who inhabited the country in the vicinity of Neah Bay, Washington. The visiting war-canoes numbered 210, with an average of twelve Indians to a canoe. The Mackah tribe, in common with the Songish and other tribes along the Island and Mainland Coasts, have nearly all disappeared. Of the great Hydahs, the Tsimpseans, the Bella Bellas, the Bella Coolas, the Nootkas, the Clayoquots, the Stickeens, and the Chilcats, only miserable remnants are to be found.

The Hudson's Bay Company's records show that both coasts were studded here and there with thickly populated villages. Previous to 1858 there must have been 150,000 Indians on the Island and Mainland Coasts. Twelve years afterwards the number throughout the entire province was estimated at 140,000. (The 1881 census showed an Indian population of 25,661.) I venture to say that between 1858 and 1870 at least 100,000 natives perished directly from the use of alcoholic stimulants supplied them by illicit vendors. It is a bold statement to make, but I feel confident that I am under rather than over the mark.

Typical of the fate of many was "Captain" John. He was Chief of the Hydahs (Haidas), then the most powerful of all the Northern Coast tribes. At one time it was estimated by the Hudson's Bay Company officials that "Captain John" had three thousand warriors under his command. When I first saw him he was about forty years of age and above the average height of an Indian. His sallow face was surrounded by luxuriant black whiskers and his upper lip was adorned with a sweeping black moustache. His stature and his light complexion and the hirsute appendages gave rise to the impression that he was the son of a Russian and an Indian woman. Perhaps he was, but his origin was shrouded in doubt.

It was a fact that when a youth he was taken to St. Petersburg in one of the Russian trading ships and that he remained there two years. Afterwards he was turned loose in London and contrived to get back to the Coast in one of the Hudson's Bay Company's ships. How he became chief I never heard. He always claimed to have been born in Alaska. He could read and write English a little, but his language was a puzzling maze of Russian, English, Chinook and Indian. With the aid of pantomimic gestures and broken words he managed to make himself understood. He was always well clad, and winter and summer wore a long blue military overcoat. His head was crowned with a blue cloth cap, around which was wound a heavy band of gold lace. When accosted by strangers his invariable custom was to point to his cap with his forefinger and exclaim, "Me big Chief," and then stalk away with an air of gloomy grandeur intended to impress the visitors with his importance.

There was much that was absurd about "Captain John's" appearance, but, taken for all in all, he was the finest specimen of the Indian I ever met. He ruled his subjects arbitrarily, and it was death or severe punishment to any member of the tribe who might disobey his orders. The Hudson's Bay Company officials knew how to manage and control the native tribes, and they gave John to understand that they depended upon him to maintain order amongst his clansmen. It is possible that he was in the Company's pay; but one thing is certain, to Captain John the whites who came here during the first rush of gold were indebted for their immunity from harm. The entire waterfront on the west side of Victoria harbor was then occupied by Indians — mostly Hydahs and Stickeens from far up the coast.

On one occasion, in the summer of 1860, the Hydah youths became very restless. They had imbibed "hiyou" (whiskey) and wanted to fight the whites. John told them they were fools — that the whites would drive them off the face of the earth. "But," said he, "if you must fight, why not attack the Stickeens?"

The Stickeens were a rival tribe that had erected their huts on the harbour front not far from where the E. & N. swing-bridge spans Victoria harbour. So that evening a drunken Hydah, observing a little Stickeen boy pass along the road, attacked him with a knife and nearly severed the child's head. Upon the discovery of the corpse the war-drums were beaten, the natives daubed their faces with paint, and the women began to sing the weird songs that always presaged an outbreak of hostilities.

The hostile tribes entrenched themselves on rocky points that overlook a small cove on the west side of Victoria harbour, above the railway bridge. Take a horseshoe and the two ends will represent the spots chosen by the tribes for their respective fortifications, and the space between will represent the cove. The natives dug pits and felled trees, from the shelter of which they peppered away at each other through the interstices of the logs. For a few days the authorities did nothing to quell the miniature war. Although several of the belligerents were wounded, none were killed, so far as was known. The third day of the conflict was Sunday, and in the afternoon, in company with several other foolish young fellows, I walked over to the Hydah "fort" to see Captain John.

We watched our opportunity, and by keeping well behind the standing timber that then thickly covered the reserve, and dodging from tree to tree, managed to reach the Captain's quarters without injury. We found the Chieftain and about a dozen of his warriors in the pit busily engaged in watching for opportunities to shoot their enemies, who were similarly employed. Every little while the sharp crack of a musket or rifle would be heard, and then a bullet would bury itself with a loud "ping!" in the earth or logs that formed the breastwork.

While there was really no danger if one kept within the "fort," the passage through the trees was hazardous. The Captain chided us for coming, but he was anxious to know what the papers said about the fight. I told him, much to his satisfaction, that they reported that he was getting the better of the Stickeens. He was very grave and serious in his demeanor, and seemed to feel that a great responsibility rested upon him. We waited until sundown before leaving the shelter of the logs. On our way back we encountered two men who were supporting a third. The latter appeared to be in pain, for he was moaning piteously.

"What is the matter?" was asked.

"One of those Stickeen bullets has gone through his leg," was the reply, "and we're helping him to town."

One of our party had had a little experience with wounds. He wrapped a handkerchief about the leg above the spot from which the blood oozed, and with a piece of wood made a sort of

Captain John during the "little war" with the Stickeen Indians in Victoria's inner harbour: "Every little while the sharp crack of a musket or rifle would be heard."

tourniquet. He drew the handkerchief so tightly that the blood soon ceased to flow, and we managed to get him to the hospital. The next day Drs. Helmcken and Trimble amputated the shattered leg above the knee. The last time I saw the unfortunate man he was limping about on one leg and a crutch.

The police department was stirred to action by this untoward event, and the constables, with a reserve force of heavily armed marines from HMS *Hecate*, proceeded to the spot, destroyed the fortifications, and arrested the principal men. Among those seized was Captain John. The leaders were soundly lectured, cautioned not to repeat their conduct, and sent back to their respective camps.

For some time peace reigned at the reserve. I have always believed that it would never have been broken at all had it not been for the unlimited quantity of strong drink with which the natives were supplied. The so-called whiskey was the vilest stuff that the ingenuity of wicked-minded and avaricious white men ever concocted. What it was composed of was known only to the concocters. I was told that it was made of alcohol, diluted with water, toned up with an extract of red pepper, and colored so as to resemble the real thing. It was conveyed to the reserve under cover of night by boatloads.

What the Indian wanted was something hot — something that would burn holes through his unaccustomed stomach and never stop burning until it reached his heels. Quality was not considered. The rotgut must be cheap as well as pungent, and those two elements being present the sale was rapid and profitable. An Indian's love of strong drink was so keen that he would sell his wife or his children into worse than slavery to obtain the money to buy it. No sacrifice was too great, no price too high to gratify his appetite for the inebriating bowl.

Several of these so-called "importing" wholesale liquor establishments were the headquarters, the manufactures, where most of the vile liquid was made and sold by a bottle or a thousand gallons at a time. Several large fortunes were made from this awful traffic.

Did the police know that this infamous business was being carried on under their eyes and noses? The answer is that they were well aware of the methods by which the Indians were being cleared off the face of the earth. They knew that the hot stuff for which a dollar a bottle was paid by the Indians did not cost the maker ten cents. The maker and seller could well afford to cut the profits in two and still realize handsomely.

For the makers and dealers to refuse to divide meant exposure and ruin for men who went to church regularly or occupied a good position in society. Did they divide? While it cannot be said with any certainty that they did, it was a notorious fact that certain firms were never disturbed. They were immune from the visits of constables. Justice was not alone blind — she was so deaf that she could not hear the plaintive cries of the wretched victims of man's greed and rapacity as they rent the night air and seemed to call down heaven's vengeance upon their poisoners. This is no fancy sketch.

Many men and women recall the awful scenes of debauchery, outrage and death that were enacted on the reserve and all along the Island and Mainland Coasts, because fire-water was ladled out to the savages in unlimited quantities. Is it any wonder that the grave-digger found frequent employment at all the Indian reserves, and that sometimes now when a posthole or a cellar is dug, the bones of the wretched people who perished before the withering blast of the illegal liquor traffic are turned up?

But back to Captain John and the Hydah. In a few weeks the lesson inculcated by the officials faded from the Indian mind, and Captain John's drunken wards grew pugnacious and drunken again. Captain John, who formerly had been noted for his sobriety, yielded at last to temptation and became an imbiber of the destroying liquid. It was even said that for a money consideration he connived the sale of spirits to his tribe, and soon pandemonium reigned supreme all over the reserve. Outrages multiplied and deaths became more frequent. A man or woman perfectly well in the morning, filled up with liquor in the afternoon, and by nightfall was carried dead from his or her lodge. The craving spread to children. Boys and girls, following the example of their elders, drank the "liquid damnation" and died, sometimes with the bottle to their lips.

A negro named Jasper walked past the Hydah reserve one afternoon and a drunken boy stabbed him to death. The boy was hanged on Bastion Square. How piteously he sobbed as he ascended the scaffold! A number of Indians witnessed the execution. They were told it was intended as an example and a warning to them to do no murder.

What hideous mockery! If the officers of the law had not allowed the liquor to be sold, there would have been no murder, and a man visiting the villages would have been as secure from harm as if he were in the streets of Victoria. A gambler who visited the reserve was set upon by natives, and in self-defence shot and killed one of his assailants. A Royal marine, strolling along the public road one evening, was attacked by Hydahs and his head nearly cut from his body. A peaceful citizen crossing a lot after dark was killed and robbed by intoxicated natives. King Freezy, monarch of the Flathead tribe, in a fit of drunken jealousy decapitated one of his wives, and soon afterwards was

An Indian village at Cowichan similar to the one
destroyed by the gunboat HMS *Forward*.

upset while in his canoe, and drowned. A canoe with three
Indians was capsized and all were drowned.

His Majesty's gunboat *Forward* proceeded to Cowichan to
quell an Indian outbreak. The vessel was fired upon and one of
the sailors killed. A terrible punishment was inflicted upon the
Indians. Their village was blown to pieces and numbers of them
killed by the ship's guns. A British bark was wrecked near Clayoquot on the west coast of Vancouver Island. The officers and
crew got safely ashore, but were murdered by the Indians,
headed by a drunken chief. [See next chapter.]

All along the coast the horrid traffic went on unchecked.
Sloops, canoes and schooners, laden at Victoria, touched at all
the villages and sold the Indians liquor which was dignified by
the name of "tanglefoot." The Indians died like flies, and soon
tribes that numbered thousands were reduced to a few score. The
scenes enacted were too awful to be told. I might continue to cite
tragedy after tragedy which resulted directly from the sale of

liquor to the poor red man by white men who worked under the actual protection of the constabulary. The instances I have given, however, will suffice to show the conditions that prevailed in and about this Christian town, beneath the shadow of church spires and within ear-shot and stone's throw of the peaceful and happy homes of pioneer settlers.

Affairs went from bad to worse. Men's lives were not considered safe when the inflammable bowl flowed at the reserve. Captain John was fast becoming a besotted, quarrelsome creature in place of the fine-looking and dignified man he was formerly. Then an event occurred which put an end to his career, although it did not stop the sale of liquor to Indians. That went on just the same, and was continued until the powerful tribes domiciled here were reduced to mere remnants, and all that was noble and good in the survivors had been burned out.

The sufferings of the tribes encamped near Victoria have never been fully described. They cannot be. It is beyond the power of the ablest pen-painter to convey to the understanding of readers of the present day a graphic description of the misery and woe that follows the trail of the Indian whiskey-seller. No more horrid scenes were enacted anywhere on this round globe than were seen on the Victoria Harbour reserve. A perfect carnival of crime, with which the authorities would not or could not cope, went on for years. But let a drunken Indian commit an offence and he was quickly punished by the strong arm of the law. No mercy was shown him.

One day, for instance, a small schooner called the *Royal Charlie*, sailing out of the harbour, was treated to a volley of musket balls fired from the Hydah village. Several shots entered the hull, and the schooner returned to the wharf. Officers were sent to the village. They arrested Captain John and a sub-chief and brought them to the police barracks. Preparatory to being placed in the cells they were being searched, when John drew a knife and made several thrusts at a constable, who promptly shot him dead. The chief's brother also drew a knife and tried to cut another constable. He, too, was shot and died instantly. Half an hour later I saw both men lying where they had fallen.

Captain John's face was covered by his lace-bound cap — the cap of which he was so proud — and his body lay beneath the navy-blue overcoat. I raised the cap and gazed long at the features, which were placid and peaceful in death. Something of the old-time nobleness lingered there and his coal-black eyes, which were still open, seemed to gaze sadly, if not reproachfully, into mine.

The *John Bright* Massacre

The uncontrolled alcohol trade resulted in the deaths of not only Indians but also of white settlers and sailors.

In December 1868 there sailed into Port Discovery, Washington, a handsome English bark named the *John Bright*. The captain, who was named Burgess, was part owner. On board were his pretty young wife and baby boy, and an English nurse maid on whose cheeks the "rosies and posies" of her native land bloomed. The vessel was a long time in loading, the facilities for quick dispatch being poor.

While the bark was taking on cargo, the captain and his wife became well acquainted on shore, and through their geniality and hospitality soon grew to be general favorites. The nurse-maid was about seventeen. Her name was Beatrice Holden. She had the lovely English complexion, bright blue eyes, and long hair of tawny hue. Pretty girls were scarce on the Sound at that time. As a result, when the day came for the bark to go to sea this particular girl received no less than three offers of marriage. She declined all with merry laughter, remarking that she intended to live and die an old maid; but should she change her mind she would only marry an Englishman.

The vessel sailed away, and passed out of the strait into the open sea early in March 1869. She was bound for Australia. The weather was boisterous, and the bark was unable to keep off shore. After a gallant struggle she was cast ashore on the island coast at a point about fourteen miles north of Clayoquot Sound.

Captain Christenson commanded at the time the trading schooner *Surprise*. The schooner was making one of her customary voyages and, word reaching the captain that a vessel had gone ashore, he sailed at once for the scene. He was some days in getting to the scene. By that time the wreck was complete, the vessel lying broadside on the shore, and the sea making a clean breach over her. The captain saw the chiefs of the tribe, and they told him that all hands were lost in the surf.

They showed him the remains of a woman (the captain's wife) with long hair lying on the beach, and Captain Christenson buried the body. He searched, but found no other remains. From some word a native let fall and from the evasive answers of the Indians generally, Captain Christenson suspected that there had been foul play. He wrote at once to Victoria of the wreck, adding that he believed some of the ship's company got ashore alive, and that they had been either murdered by the Indians or were held in captivity at some place well back from the shore. Mr. Seymour, who was then Governor, was told of the captain's suspicions, and was asked to send a war vessel to the scene. He declined to act, expressing the belief that all hands had perished. Three weeks passed and nothing was done. Captain Christenson could not rest easy. Despairing of government assistance, at great personal risk he again visited the scene of the wreck.

He walked along the shore — the very shore over which he had walked three weeks before — and to his horror discovered other bodies of white men lying above high-water mark. The remains had been frightfully mangled. In every case the head was missing, having been cut off to preclude the possibility of identification. In some instances an arm or leg was missing. The fast-decaying bodies had been stripped of all clothing, and no trace was ever found of the baby. The captain again wrote, and the facts were laid before the Governor, whose dilatory course caused the massacre. H.M.S. *Sparrowhawk* was directed to proceed to the coast.

The party landed at the nearest safe harbour to the scene of the wreck, and the shore was searched. Nine dead bodies, decapitated and mangled in the manner I have stated, were found. It was shown afterwards that the captain had been shot through

Governor Frederick Seymour refused to send a gunboat to the scene of the massacre.

133

the back while in the act of running away in the vain hope of escaping from the cruel savages, who had proved themselves to be less merciful than the wild waves. The other prisoners were thrown down and their heads removed while they piteously begged for mercy! The natives were questioned, and at first denied all knowledge of how the bodies came there. But when confronted with Christenson's evidence they confessed that the entire ship's company got safely ashore. The Indians were drunk and in a dangerous mood. The captain's wife and one seaman were killed the first day. The pretty English maid was delivered up to the young men of the tribe, who dragged her into the bush. Her cries filled the air for hours. When she was seen again by one of the native witnesses some hours later, the poor girl was dead, and her head had disappeared! Her body was not found by the officers, although a diligent search was instituted. Her sad fate appealed to the hearts of the officials and stirred their indignation, and they desired to give her remains a Christian burial.

The witnesses further disclosed that the captain and the rest of the survivors were secreted in the bush, and were alive and within a few hundred yards of Christenson when he first reached the scene. They saw him, too, and were threatened with instant death if they dared to make an outcry. After Christenson's departure the tribe waited several days, fearing the warships would come, and they hesitated to murder the survivors. At last the savages pretended they had secured passage for the men on a liquor schooner that had just discharged her cargo and was sailing for Victoria. They lured the poor people to the shore where they were cruelly massacred, and their bodies left where they fell.

Several Indians were seized and brought to Victoria. They were tried, and two of the number were convicted. The culprits were taken to the scene of their crime in the *Sparrowhawk* and, in the presence of the whole tribe, were hanged. The scaffold was left standing as a warning to other evil-disposed Indians who might be inclined to ill-treat other crews that should be cast on their shore.

The lesson proved salutary. A year or two later the bark *Edwin*, commanded by Captain S.A. Hughes, dropped anchor in Royal Roads. The captain had his wife and two bright little boys, aged seven and nine years, on board. Accompanied by his wife and children, Captain Hughes came ashore at Victoria and did some shopping. In the evening he set sail for California with a cargo of lumber. Three days later the bark encountered a severe gale. The sails split as if made of paper, and soon the vessel was being swept towards the rocky shore. Every effort was made to keep her off, but wind and waves were too powerful. She struck nearly in the identical spot where the *John Bright* laid her bones. Mrs. Hughes, the two children and two seamen were swept overboard, and drowned almost immediately. Captain Hughes and the remainder of the crew managed to reach the shore, landing almost at the foot of the scaffold on which the murderers were hanged. The Indians received them with kindness and hospitality, and showered favors upon the men. To those who had no clothes they contributed from their own scanty store. Captain Christenson brought the shipwrecked men to Victoria in the *Surprise*. Captain Hughes landed without a penny in his pockets or an acquaintance in the town. To a reporter he said:

"I never was in such a fix before in all my life. Ten days ago I had a wife and two children, was the owner of a neat little clipper bark, and had $5,000 in my cabin. I didn't owe a cent to anyone. Today," he added, and his eyes filled with tears and lips quivered, "I am destitute of wife and children and money, and am thrown on the world a beggar. A man had better be dead. How I wish the sea had swallowed me up, too!"

"Cheer up," said the reporter, "there are plenty of men here who will aid you."

"That's just it," he replied, "I don't want to accept favors from anyone. And yet I've seen the day when I was able to help, and did help, a shipwrecked crew."

"When was that?" was asked.

"It was in the mid-Atlantic," he replied. "The ship *Aquilla* was flying signals of distress. I hailed her, and was told that the ship was sinking. I stood by and took off Captain Sayward and all his men, and carried them to New York. The United States Congress voted me this gold watch and chain."

He drew the watch from his pocket. Opening the case, he showed an inscription which ran something like this:

"Presented to Captain S.A. Hughes, of the British bark *Gertrude*, as a mark of appreciation for his gallant conduct in saving the lives of Captain Sayward and the crew of the American ship *Aquilla*."

It did not take many minutes for the information to pass from mouth to mouth that the man who had saved the life of one of Victoria's best known citizens was in need of assistance. The best that could be had was not deemed too good for Captain Hughes.

It is worthy of remark that never since the lesson taught the tribes on the West Coast have shipwrecked people been molested. In fact, the natives have been ever foremost in saving life, and in some instances have rescued and brought crews to Victoria.

A Fugitive from Justice

For their friend, the author and Frank Way imperilled their own safety and broke the law. The result was "disenchanting."

In August 1858, there came to Yale a young man and his wife. The couple were genteel-looking, had evidently been accustomed to good society, spoke like people of culture, and, what was better than all in some eyes, they had much money. They also had a girl of about seven — sweet, pretty and petite, a perfect fairy, with lovely blue eyes and light hair, and such winsome ways! The mother was a most engaging conversationalist. She had travelled in Europe with her father and mother and had a wealth of anecdotes and scenery to tell and describe. They gave the name of Gregory, and claimed to have come from a small city in the interior of New York State.

Gregory bought a cabin on the second bench back of Yale which belonged to Mr. McRoberts, a Scotch gentleman, who, with his wife, occupied a larger and better cottage near the Court House. The Gregorys furnished their home neatly and comfortably with such articles as they were able to procure at the Hudson's Bay Store, then managed by Mr. Allard, chief trader. He was a French-Canadian and one of the best friends I ever had. John Kurtz, Hugh Nelson, Walter Gladwin and myself, all former San Franciscans, had crystallized and formed a little club, or set of our own, to which we admitted Mr. Kelly, the lawyer from Australia, and a few other kindred spirits.

The Gregorys, when they first came to the camp, were reserved and "offish" in manner, and seemed to shrink from observation. I became acquainted with them in rather an odd manner. The water supply of the inhabitants was conveyed from the river to the houses and stores in buckets. The Indians were the water-carriers, and every morning and evening a bucket-brigade of natives was engaged in packing water from the river to the people who lived on the benches.

One morning, very early, I was busy outside my place. I saw Mrs. Gregory, in a loose wrapper and without her crinoline, carrying a huge pitcher in her hands, pass down towards the river bank. With no object save the gratification of a natural interest which a pretty woman usually arouses in a young fellow just out of his teens, I watched her as she carefully picked her way over and around the boulders on the bar. When she had filled the pitcher and started back I still kept her in view.

I would gladly have asked her permission to get the water for her, but as we were not acquainted I feared that the offer might be regarded as an impertinence. The lady was threading her way along the rock-beset path when suddenly her foot slipped. Down she went on her knees, the pitcher breaking and the water splashing over her. I ran into my tent and, seizing a towel and a bucket, flew down the trail to where the lady stood drenched and looking very woebegone. I handed her the towel as I passed and, running on to the river, filled the bucket.

When I returned she had used the towel to some effect, but the dress of thin material, wet through and through, clung closely and set off her shapely figure. She blushed like a red, red rose. As I approached she stammered a few words of thankfulness, adding, "What shall I do for some water? Charley is too sick to come himself for it, and the Indian carrier did not call last night?"

"Why," I said, "I filled this bucket for you. If you will permit me and will walk behind me (I did not think she would be pleased, with the wet dress hanging closely to her form, to walk in front) I will carry it to your house."

"Oh! thank you," she said, "I am more than obliged for your kindness."

At the time of which I write a lady who should have appeared in public in a habit that fitted closely to her figure and a shirt waist would have been looked upon with suspicion, at least. The aim of fashion was to hide as much of the female "form divine" as possible. The women of that period actually walked about in wire cages, which hung suspended from their waists and concealed the outlines of their bodies and limbs. Remove the pan of a circular birdcage and retain the wire part and you will have a very fair idea of the article our mothers and sweethearts moved about in 1858.

In a few minutes we reached the cabin. The little girl, with her hair in curl-papers, was in the kitchen and immediately came up and put her hand confidingly in mine. We were friends in an instant. I inquired if I could do anything else to assist, but Mrs.

Gregory declined any further aid and I withdrew.

That afternoon the little girl came to my cabin with a note from her mother asking me if I would summon a doctor, as her husband seemed very ill. I called in Dr. Fifer, a near neighbor. In a day or two the patient was about again, apparently as well as ever. When the couple called with the little girl to thank me for my assistance, we had a good laugh over the broken pitcher incident.

Of course, the Gregorys joined our little club and proved to be among its most valuable and interesting members. When winter evenings set in and snow lay on the ground, and the cold blasts roared through the deep recesses of the canyons and moaned and shrieked about our frail habitations, we only piled higher the logs in the fire-place. As the ruddy flames cast a warm glow over the little party of friends, we bade defiance to the fuming and raging of the Storm King.

The winter of 1858-59 slipped rapidly away. Spring found us all alive and as happy as possible under the circumstances of remoteness from the outer world and a sometimes short supply of wholesome food. The Gregorys had become the most popular people in the village, and the little girl — Mae Judith — was welcomed everywhere. I named one of my claims "Little Judy" in her honor.

One evening when Nelson and I were seated on a rude bench in front of the Gregory cabin I observed an old gentleman advancing up the bank. When he reached the top he halted for a moment to gaze upon the magnificent panorama of snow-clad hills which stretched into space on all sides. Then he strolled along until he came opposite to us. Addressing Mr. Nelson, he asked if he would direct him to Yale Creek. Mr. Nelson pointed in the direction and the old gentleman, bowing politely, passed on.

The next day I met him on the main street, walking listlessly along, gazing at the stores, the cabins and the rushing river alternately. An hour or so afterwards I found myself seated at the same table with him at Wm. Power's Hotel. We soon struck up an acquaintance, and he told me that his name was Merrill, that he was a resident of Philadelphia, and sufficiently well-to-do to travel for pleasure. "I am not rich," he added, "but I have enough."

He was tall and apparently 60 years of age. His hair was snow-white and he wore a full white beard close cut. He was dressed as a gentleman of the period in clothes of fashionable make. Taken all in all, he was what the ladies would call "a nice-looking old gentleman." He explained that he was travelling for his health and, being an ardent fisherman, had already made a slight acquaintance with the trout in Yale Creek. The following afternoon found us both casting the fly in the creek. Merrill caught two fish to my one, and when the shades of evening began to gather we counted our catch and found that we had a dozen plump trout. On our way in I proposed that we should present Mrs. Gregory with the catch. Merrill was not acquainted with the Gregorys, but when I made the presentation Mr. Gregory invited us inside. The ice being thus broken, the newcomer was immediately accepted as a welcome guest.

From that time on the intimacy grew, and it was an almost daily occurrence for the couple to receive a few trout or a brace of grouse from Mr. Merrill or myself. Our little club continued to meet at the different homes and had a good time generally. Mr. Merrill, having joined us, added much to our enjoyment and pleasure by his exquisite playing on the flute and his rendition of some of the old songs in a low and sweet tenor voice. We became very much attached to him. Although each week he would announce that the next week he would leave for home, he lingered on and on and became more and more intimate at the Gregorys'.

"Can't you see what's the matter?" asked Kurtz one day, as we were discussing Merrill's prolonged stay.

"I'm sure I can't," said I.

"Well, I'll tell you, then. He's gone on Mrs. Gregory."

"Nonsense," I returned. "He's an old man and she's not more than twenty-two."

"I don't care. He's gone on her," insisted Kurtz.

In a day or two I became convinced that the dainty little lady had really captivated Mr. Merrill, and that, perhaps all unconsciously to herself, he was being drawn more and more to her side. In fact, he did not seem happy except when loitering about the Gregory house. He was now a daily guest and almost appeared to have established himself as one of the family.

I didn't like the aspect of things at all. It was none of my business, but I felt somewhat indignant at the turn affairs had taken — indignant to think that Merrill, whom I had introduced to the family, had displaced me, as it were, in their regard.

About this time I noticed that a great change had come over my lawyer friend Kelly. He seldom went to the Gregorys now and he seldom attended the club meetings. When I met him he seemed to wish to avoid me, grew abstracted and moody in his manner, and took to walking by himself. Was he, too, the least bit jealous? Once I encountered Kelly and Merrill in deep conversation at Power's, but I thought nothing of that. And so the weeks wore on. Merrill remained, without giving any sign, except the oft repeated assertion, that he intended to go away. The club gradually became demoralized. Its meetings fell off and then ceased altogether.

"Do you know," I said to Nelson one day. "I believe that that man Merrill is no good? Who knows anything about him? Why, he may be the biggest rascal unhung for all we know. What's he doing here, anyhow?"

Nelson just laughed loud and long. "Don't be a fool," he said. "The old man's too many for you young chaps, and that's all there is about it. You're jealous and so is Kurtz, and so are all the rest. What business is it of ours if the Gregorys like him?"

Next I tried Kelly. He said nothing, but shook his head and walked off with a pensive and dejected air. So I discontinued my visits to the Gregorys and ceased to talk about them and Merrill, although whenever I met them the lady and gentleman urged me to call and evidently wondered at my continued absence.

One afternoon the Gregorys left Yale by the trail for Texas Bar, a few miles down the river. They announced that they would return late the same evening. Merrill was much concerned at their proposed absence and accompanied them some two miles on their journey. He got back late in the afternoon and, after dining, went to his room. After dark a light was seen in their cabin. The next morning Gregory complained that during their absence the cabin had been entered. Although everything had been turned topsy-turvy, nothing had been taken except a few papers. The affair created a little interest for a day or two, and was then forgotten.

Shortly afterwards, one dismal, stormy night I sat at my desk writing a letter for a San Francisco newspaper. The candle had burned low in its holder, so I blew the flickering light out and rose to procure a fresh one. As I groped towards the box I became aware, by a gentle tapping on the window-pane, of someone on the outside who wished to come in.

"Who's there?" I demanded.

The deep voice of lawyer Kelly responded in a hoarse whisper, "Let me in, Higgins. I want to speak to you. Don't light your candle. I must talk to you in the dark, or not at all. I've something to tell you. Let me in, quick, by the back door."

The lawyer stumbled rather than walked inside, closed and bolted the door and took me by the hand. I noticed that his hand trembled like an aspen leaf, and his breath came and went in great puffs like that of a man who had ascended a pair of stairs rapidly.

"Look here," he exclaimed, "I come to you for advice. I'm in a devil of a fix. I've done a most despicable thing. For money I have consented to betray a man who never did me any harm, whose hospitality I have enjoyed and whom I love like a brother."

I was shocked, frightened by his agitation and his words. Was I the friend whom he had consented to betray? By a strong effort I controlled my feelings and managed to ask: "Kelly, what in the name of all that is good and great and holy do you mean?"

"I mean that I'm a villain — that I have taken a retainer of $100 in gold to entrap and betray a friend. I'm a Judas, the only difference between me and Iscariot being that where he took silver I took gold. The principle — or rather the want of it — is the same. I wish I had died before I ever saw Yale. I've taken blood-money — blood-money!"

"Come, now," I said, soothingly, "tell me all about it. That's a good chap."

"Oh!" he groaned. "How can I tell the story of my shame, my disgrace, my fall."

"If you don't tell me," I urged, "how can I help and advise you."

"That's right," he said. "I must tell you. Well, that Merrill's a devil."

Instantly, it occurred to me that there had been trouble at the Gregory household. The old man had either flown with the pretty little woman or had insulted her, and Kelly had been retained to defend Merrill, and now repented of having taken the fee.

"I knew it, I knew it!" I eagerly exclaimed. "He's no good, and I said so weeks ago."

"No," broke in Kelly, "you're wrong — at least it's not in the way you think. Gregory is a defaulter. He was cashier in a New York bank, and was short in his accounts to an enormous amount. He came here to hide. Merrill is a great detective — the greatest in America. He followed him here and has stayed ever since, accepting his hospitality, eating his salt, and awaiting an opportunity to take him back. But the extradition treaty is so lame and faulty that it does not cover this case, and Merrill has been awaiting a chance for months to induce Gregory to set his foot on American soil where he can be seized.

"The detective consulted me and I told him he could not take his quarry back legally, but that if he could get him across the line he might kidnap him. I consented to act as a spy on my friend and entrap him, and leave his dear wife and that sweet little Mae unprotected. My God! (beating his brow with his clenched fist) I am the most miserable wretch in Yale tonight. I have been most wretched ever since I yielded to temptation. What shall I do?"

"Pay back the money and retire from the case," I cried.

"Oh, but the worst is not yet told. Tomorrow morning Gregory and Merrill will leave for Point Roberts where, the detective has told him, he has a gold mine, but where the defaulter will be laid hold of as a criminal. A canoe with an Indian crew has been engaged and the supplies are on board. It lies on the river bank and at daybreak they will be off. At the last moment I have come to you. My conscience is awakened. Just think of my aiding a scheme to rob that woman and her child of their protector and send him to prison. What can be done to save him and make me a decent white man again?"

I thought for a few moments and then said, "We must tell others and get their assistance to counter-act this infamous scheme."

"But," said Kelly, "what becomes of my honor, my sworn pledge as a barrister? How can I save my friend without betraying my client? And if I betray my client Chief Justice Begbie will strike me off the rolls."

"The detective had no right to ask you to assist him in an infamous transaction, and it is not professional in you to retain a fee for doing dirty work. Throw the fee back and let me tell Kurtz and Nelson all about the plot."

"You are right," said Kelly, after a pause. "Do as you wish."

"Wait here till I return," I said. I opened the door cautiously and peered out. No one was in sight, and I soon found myself in the room with John Kurtz and Hugh Nelson.

Seated in a chair was Frank Way, who conducted the Spuzzum ferry where the Trutch Suspension Bridge was afterwards erected. Frank was a droll character. He was an American and not a man of much education, but he was as bright as a new sovereign. During the gold rush he made barrels of money by ferrying miners and their effects across the Fraser River at fifty cents a head. He told me that one day he earned in fares a tin bucket full of silver and gold. Once, he said, he started across with ten men in his boat. The craft ran into a riffle and was upset. All were precipitated into the water, and all were drowned save him.

I laid Kelly's trouble before the three friends, and we all agreed that the situation was a serious one and that if Gregory was to be saved immediate action must be taken. Several plans were suggested and abandoned because they involved the telling to the woman the story of her husband's shame. We assumed that she did not know of it, and we wished to spare her that trial.

At last Frank Way asked, "Where did Kelly say the canoe is moored?"

"In front of the bar, and the supplies are already on board. The party will leave at the first glimmer of daylight."

"Humph!" said Frank, thoughtfully. Then rising and yawning as if weary of the whole business, he beckoned to me and we took our leave. Way remained outside of my house while I went in and told Kelly that all were of the opinion that the retainer should be returned, and that if at daybreak no other solution could be found, Mrs. Gregory must be told and the plot exposed. The lawyer eagerly accepted the proposition to return the fee, but he shrank from the publicity that would attach to the transaction. As there was bad blood between himself and Chief Justice Begbie, he dreaded the outcome should the matter reach the Chief Justice's ears.

Aurora's rosy fingers had just pinned back the sable curtains of night, and the eastern sky showed signs of the approach of another day, when Gregory left his cabin and threaded his way towards the beach. As he walked on, the unsuspecting man hummed a popular air, happy in the anticipation of sudden wealth and assured prosperity. As he neared the river he saw the tall form of Merrill running excitedly up and down in the dim light, berating the crew of Indians who had been employed to navigate the boat to the mouth of the river. When he saw Gregory, Merrill cried: "Come here, quick!"

Gregory hastened his steps and soon saw the cause of Merrill's anger. During the night someone with an axe had cut and hacked the canoe until it was practically destroyed. The supplies that were laid in overnight must have been thrown into the river, for they were nowhere to be seen.

Merrill was in a fearful rage. All his gentlemanly reserve was gone and his mouth emitted the most frightful profanity. He abused the Indian crew and fiercely turned on Gregory and accused him of being in the plot to destroy the canoe.

Gregory denied all knowledge of the affair.

"I never knew a thief who was not a liar," exclaimed Merrill.

"What do you mean?" hotly asked Gregory.

"I mean that you are a thief — and you know it, and I know it!"

Gregory fell back as if struck a hard blow.

"Yes," screamed the detective, his anger growing hotter and hotter. "You robbed a bank in New York City. Your name is no more Gregory than my name's Merrill. If you were on the American side I would arrest you as a common thief. You are safe here, but I'll get you yet!"

Gregory, crushed and broken by the tirade of abuse and the knowledge of his crime so unexpectedly launched at him by the detective, walked slowly away in one direction, while Merrill started to walk rapidly off in another. In his excitement the detective had not remembered the Indian crew. They, four in number, and armed with paddles, ran after him and demanded pay for their wrecked vessel. He tried to pass on, but they obstructed his path and loudly demanded compensation, which at last he reluctantly gave them.

When Merrill and Gregory had passed out of sight two heads were raised above a great boulder. After a careful survey the heads were followed by the bodies of two young white men who walked to the beach and gazed at the wreck and expressed sympathy for the owners of the craft. Then the two walked slowly back to town, chuckling and laughing as they went, and sought their respective couches. They had been out all night and needed a little rest.

At noon Merrill, Kurtz and I met at Power's. Merrill had calmed down by this time, and his manner was as placid and serene as usual. He had no reason to think that we knew aught of the affair of the early morning.

"Mr. Merrill," Kurtz said, "I am commissioned by a gentleman who says he is indebted to you to give you $100 in gold."

Merrill started slightly and then said, "I was not aware I had a debtor in the camp. What is his name?"

"Kelly," I broke in, excitedly. "He says you employed him to do some legal business for you, but instead you tried to convert him into a detective. He declines to degrade the legal profession in that manner and returns your retainer."

Merrill, who saw that his disguise had been penetrated and his designs were known, took the money without another word and gave a receipt. In the body of the receipt I was careful to introduce the words which made it clear that Kelly had taken the retainer under a misapprehension, so, should Begbie hear of the affair (which he never did), no harm could have resulted to my friend. Merrill, unable to secure his prey, the following day left the river and Yale knew him no more. The papers stolen from Gregory's house were never recovered.

Some ten years later in July 1868, I found myself walking along an up-town street in New York City. As I walked along I suddenly became conscious that my name had been called by some person behind me. I turned and saw a lady and gentleman, dressed in the extreme of fashion, and at their side a tall, elegant-looking young lady of about seventeen.

"How do you do?" asked the lady.

"I'm well, thank you," I replied suspiciously, for I had heard of the confidence men and women of New York who pick up and swindle greenies by pretending to have known them in other parts.

"Do you not recognize us?" asked the gentleman.

"I certainly do not," I rejoined, still suspicious.

"Do you not remember the Gregorys at Yale?"

"Yes, indeed I do," and then a light dawned upon me. These

were my old-time friends. We shook hands, but the Gregorys' grasp was anything but cordial. Their hands lay in mine like dead fish. Then the maiden came forward and bowed distantly.

"And this, I suppose, is my dear little friend, Mae Judith — little Judy," I exclaimed joyously.

"I am Miss Gregory," she said, with an emphasis on the Miss.

Yes, she was the same girl whom I often held on my knee, and for whom I had invented appalling stories of fire and shipwreck and fairies and hobgoblins in the days of old, the days of gold. She had grown tall and graceful, with the same lovely eyes and the fair hair turned a little darker, but still a beautiful sun-kissed blonde.

"I remember you very well," she continued. "I shall never forget the nice trout you used to bring us."

"And I," said Mrs. Gregory, "always recall the pitcher of water that splashed over me when I think of you."

"Yes," I said, "those were occasions to be remembered."

I turned to Gregory. I wondered if he could recall anything more substantial that I had done for him and his. All he had to say was, "What could I get for my two lots at Yale?"

Not a word of gratitude or thanks for the man who, with Frank Way, had imperilled his own safety and committed an offence under the law to prevent him falling into the hands of justice. I told them the latest news about their former neighbors and then with a sort of cold-storage air we parted forever. I was disenchanted.

To be remembered only for a few trout and a broken pitcher, after the tremendous sacrifice I had made for them, was too much for my sensitive nature. I dropped the curtain on the episode. What Gregory's right name was, or how the man got out of the financial stress, I did not know, nor did I care to inquire. I never heard of them again, and have managed to survive the estrangement.

The 1860s Cariboo gold rush yielded
treasure by the ton, with remarkably few
robberies. An exception was

The Wrong Saddlebags

Early in May 1856, a British steamship sailed from Southampton,
bound for the West Indies. Amongst her three or four hundred
passengers were a young couple, Mr. and Mrs. George Storm.
They gave out that they had been recently married, and from
their appearance they were well-bred and well connected. The
pretty bride, who was little more than a girl, was exceedingly
pleasant in her manners, and made friends of all with whom she
came in contact. Among the acquaintances they made was a
middle-aged gentleman named William Stephenson.

He was an Englishman and, having been to California, was
on his way back to look after some mines that he owned there.
As Mr. and Mrs. Storm were also bound to California, they found
the information which Mr. Stephenson possessed of the country
most valuable. So the three were thrown much together, and by
the time the steamer reached the Isthmus of Darien they had
become fast friends and had formed plans for the future. In due
course, the passengers crossed the Isthmus (today the Panama
Canal) and embarked on a steamer which landed them at San
Francisco. Here Mr. Stephenson learned that the bank in which
he had on deposit a large sum of money had failed. A project
which he had in view for the advancement of his new-found
friends could not be carried out.

The Storms were naturally greatly disappointed at the result,
as they were not overburdened with means. After some days,
they departed for the interior of the State, where Storm said he
would try his luck at the diggings. They took leave of each other,
Stephenson remaining at San Francisco to recover what he could
from the bank failure. A fact which struck Stephenson as strange

To safeguard gold shipments, in 1861 the government formed an armed escort, above in Barkerville in 1863. The escort wasn't a success and was disbanded after three trips. Stagecoaches carried most of the gold, with one safely bringing $600,000 in a single trip, treasure worth some $18 million at today's price of gold. Not until 1890 was there a robbery when Martin Van Rowland held up the stage near 100 Mile House. He escaped with $4,500 in gold but was caught and sentenced to a jail term.

Hurdy-gurdy dancers at Barkerville in 1868. They were not prostitutes but "working girls" who for $1 a minute danced with the miners then led them to the bar where the girls received a commission on the drinks.

was that the Storms had not a single letter of introduction as to their connections or antecedents, beyond the fact that their match was a runaway one and that the girl's friends objected to her marrying Storm.

But, as they were very nice, and apparently respectable, Mr. Stephenson took them entirely into his confidence, lending Storm a considerable sum of money from his depleted store. He parted from them with regret, for he well knew the temptations to which they would be subjected in the mining towns. Several years passed, during which time Stephenson did not hear from his steamship acquaintances. He at last gave up all hope of ever meeting them. Although he often wondered what had become of them, they gradually faded from his mind.

In 1862 the Cariboo gold fever broke out in the then Colony of British Columbia. Early in that year Mr. Stephenson joined in the rush to the new gold fields. The path through the then unexplored country was difficult and dangerous. Thousands walked every foot of the way and reached Williams Creek, where the richest deposits were found, weary and worn from the hardships they had gone through.

Stephenson was so fortunate as to secure a claim upon one of the richest bars on the creek. Near this bar "Old Man" Diller, Hard Curry, Bill Abbott, Jim Loring, John Kurtz, Bill Cunningham, John Adams, Wm. Farron, John A. Cameron, Bob Stevenson, and a host of others, whose names will ever live in history as the possessors of rich claims in Cariboo, were located. They washed out hundreds of thousands of dollars in a single season. Frequently, as high as $5,000 was obtained from a single bucket. When Abbott one evening staked $5,000 on a single hand at poker, and was remonstrated with for his foolishness, he replied:

"Oh, pshaw! It's only a single bucket. There's five hundred thousand such buckets still in the claim."

The day came when poor old Abbott walked the streets of a British Columbia town in search of a man who would lend him the wherewithal for a meal, and found him not. Of the hundreds who had fattened at his board in the days of his affluence, not one offered to help him when he became poor again.

Abbott's fate was that of nearly all the men who made big money in Cariboo. Cameron carried his earnings to Eastern Canada. He had $175,000. This huge sum he lost in a few years in bad speculations. Twenty-five years later he returned to the scene of his former success and opened a little eating-house. One day, while supplying a customer, he dropped dead. Old Man Diller was almost the only one who held on to his talent and made more. He settled down in Pennsylvania, where he invested in real estate and died worth an enormous sum. Bob Stevenson lost his wealth in trying to add to it.

Our steamship acquaintance, Stephenson, from whom I have obtained much of the material for this narration, returned to California. He told me that in a single season he made $56,000 on Williams Creek, and that he sold out to his partners at the close of the year for $10,000 more. Like Diller, he kept his pile, and added to it.

A day or two after Stephenson had disposed of his claim, and was popularly supposed to have a large sum in his cabin, he strolled into a gambling house at Barkerville. Gathered in the house were many evil-looking men and women. The scene was dimly lighted with kerosene lamps. On the tables were cards, dice and faro-banks, and a billiard table in the center of the room was utilized for the purposes of keno. A continual stream of miners and business men were entering and departing, after trying their luck at the different games, or imbibing at the bar.

Attracted by a sound of revelry, Stephenson next entered a long hall in which a number of miners and others were engaged in wooing the favor of Terpsichore with a number of highly perfumed and gorgeously arrayed females. They were known as hurdy-gurdy girls. These representatives of the goddess of dancing were imported from California expressly to serve as partners for the miners of Cariboo.

All were not young or beautiful, but they were very gracious, and never refused to drink when asked. Indeed, they were expected to urge their partners to treat them at the close of each dance. As the broad light of day often streamed into the hall before shutting-up time came, the amount of liquor consumed on the premises at the rate of 50 cents per drink must have been very great. As he stood gazing at the whirling figures, Stephenson witnessed a dastardly act. A ruffian who had been disappointed in obtaining the hand of one of the painted and bedizened creatures watched his opportunity. When he fancied he was not observed, he struck her violently in the face and ran toward the door. The woman screamed and would have fallen had not the strong arm of Stephenson caught her and laid her gently on the floor. A crowd gathered at once, and chase was made for the assailant, who was soon overtaken and severely beaten.

In the meantime, Stephenson busied himself in restoring the unfortunate woman to consciousness. His efforts were soon rewarded, and he had the satisfaction of seeing her open her eyes and ask to be taken to her room. She had a bad bruise on her face. As she was assisted to her feet the woman gazed long and earnestly at Stephenson.

"Where — where have I seen you before? Was it in England?

or was it in California? No, it cannot be. Surely you are not Mr. Stephenson? You are not the gentleman I met on the Southampton boat?"

"My name is Stephenson," he replied. "But I cannot recall that we ever met before."

"Am I then so changed that you do not know me?" the wretched woman asked. "Do you not remember George Storm and his wife?"

"Yes — yes — but do not tell me that you are Mrs. Storm!"

"I am that lost woman," she cried, as she burst into a flood of tears.

"And where is your husband?" Stephenson asked, with emotion.

"He is here — in this camp."

"And does he know that you," he hesitated a moment for a word, not wishing to wound the woman's feelings, and then added, "that you are here?"

"Yes, but do not blame him. We were reduced to great straits. My baby died, and my friends at home would not help us, so — and so — you know the rest."

Again the poor woman wept, and Stephenson could scarcely refrain from mingling his tears with hers. With a great effort he restrained himself. Having arranged for a surgeon to attend to her injury, he left her, promising to return on the morrow, mentally resolving to do all in his power to rescue her from her forlorn condition.

Stephenson followed the winding of the creek to his cabin, which was situated about a mile above Barkerville. The night was intensely dark. As he neared his place, he observed a light within. He approached a window and peered cautiously into the front room and plainly saw the figure of a tall man standing by the side of the bunk. He was in the act of raising one of the mattresses, apparently searching for valuables. Stephenson turned for the purpose of raising an alarm, when he became conscious of the presence of another man who advanced from the shadow of the cabin and dealt him a severe blow on the head.

The victim fell at once and lay where he fell until early morning. He was discovered by some miners on their way to work, and his injuries, which were quite severe, were attended to by Dr. Black, then a noted practitioner on Williams Creek. The doctor decided that the patient had been sandbagged, and ordered his removal to the hospital, where several days elapsed before he recovered sufficiently to tell how he received the hurt.

By that time, identification of the robbers was impossible, and no steps were ever taken to apprehend them. They got very little for their crime, as their victim had providentially deposited nearly all his wealth in the bank. As soon as Stephenson obtained his discharge from the hospital, he repaired to the dance hall and enquired for Mrs. Storm, who was known to the inmates as Bella Armitage. To his profound grief he learned that she had left the creek the day after the assault, and that a man, calling himself her husband, had gone with her.

In the fall of 1862 a great event occurred. Lord Milton accompanied by his friend and medical adviser, Dr. Cheadle, arrived on Williams Creek. They had come across the continent by the overland route and had been nearly a year on the way. Cheadle was a man of fine proportions, but Milton was only about five feet in height, and weighed scarcely one hundred and twenty pounds. However, as the saying goes, there are many good goods put up in small packages. Lord Milton was just about as genial, liberal and light-hearted a fellow as you ever met. He didn't look much like a lord though, and many amusing incidents arose through Cheadle being mistaken for the nobleman, and the lord for the doctor. The "boys" gave the visitors a big banquet, and "whooped it up" until the small hours.

Milton and Cheadle, on their return to England, wrote a most entertaining book on their travels, in which they gave a graphic description of the dinner. They were especially struck with the wit and hospitality of the late William Farron, who gave the visitors a most hearty welcome and a handful of nuggets. Mr. Farron was one of the lucky miners of that period, and realized a competency in one season.

Stephenson lingered about Barkerville until the latter part of July of the following year. He was hoping to hear from a party of prospectors under John Rose, whom he had sent out the previous fall, and who had not been heard from since their departure. When news did come in it was of the most dismal character. Rose and his party had died of exposure on one of the unexplored creeks, and their bodies were buried where they were found.

Stephenson immediately left Cariboo and travelled by easy stages toward the lower country. He was accompanied by several other miners, who, having made their pile, were desirous of reaching civilization by the speediest and safest means. As the road was believed to be infested with desperate men who had failed to win gold at the diggings, the miners kept closely together, and were fully armed. On their way out the party fell in with a young man named Tom Clegg, a clerk in the employ of E.T. Dodge & Co., merchants.

Clegg, who was on a collecting tour, was known to have in his possession a very large sum of money which he carried in saddlebags on his horse, a large, powerful animal. He was accompanied by a Captain Taylor who rode a mule. When Taylor and Clegg fell in with the miners they expressed great pleasure at the protection afforded, and agreed to keep close by them. The party reached 144 Mile House, a wayside inn, in good shape. But there they fell to drinking and carousing. When day dawned neither Clegg nor Taylor was in a fit condition to travel, so the others started without them. Clegg and Taylor followed about an hour later, having changed animals at the Post, Taylor riding the horse with the gold-laden saddlebags, and Clegg bestriding the mule which carried no treasure. A short distance below the Post two men were seen ahead. As the travellers approached the men separated, one crossing to one side and the other to the other side of the road, as if to let the horsemen pass between them. When the horsemen came opposite them, each footman grasped a bridle and began shooting.

Taylor's horse took fright, reared and broke loose, dashing the man who held him to the ground. It got clear away, darting along the road at great speed. Clegg leaped from his mule, and seized the man who held his mule's bridle. He was getting the best of the highwayman when the man who had tried to stop Taylor's horse came to the assistance of his pal and shot Clegg dead. The robbers then cut the saddlebags from the mule's back, under the impression that they contained the gold and, plunging into the thicket, disappeared.

The murderers were seen the next day by William Humphrey who was driving a light wagon along the road. While following the trail of the highwaymen through the brush the Indian trackers came upon the saddlebags. They had been cut open and the contents, a bundle of papers and a suit of underclothes, lay on the ground. What must have been the feeling of the robbers, when it dawned upon them that they had taken the life of a fellow-being, and imperilled their own lives, for so paltry a booty as the wrong saddlebags contained, may be imagined. One robber, who gave the name of Robert Armitage, was caught in the valley of the Bonaparte. The other disappeared, and was seen no more alive. For a long time it was feared that he had got out of the country. Then one morning a farmer on the North Thompson River, while watering his stock, saw on one of the bars what he at first took to be a bundle of clothes. But upon closer examination it proved to be the body of the missing highwayman. The survivor was committed for trial before that judicial terror, Judge Begbie.

Stephenson, having convoyed his gold to Yale, placed it in the hands of Billy Ballou, the pioneer expressman, for transmission to the Bank of British North America at Victoria. Leaving the express office he walked slowly along the front street, and almost the first person he met was Mrs. Storm, alias Armitage. She had recovered from the effects of the cruel blow and with her face divested of the paint, she looked like her former self. Accosting him, she said, imploringly:

"Oh, Mr. Stephenson, I am so glad to have met you, for I am in great trouble, and need your help. I have just received a letter from Mr. Storm. He is in prison at Lillooet. He is charged with the murder and robbery of a man on the Cariboo wagon road. He is without money and friends and unless he can get some money, he will surely be hanged. Will you help him?"

Stephenson told me, many years afterwards, that he at first declined to accede to the unhappy woman's appeal. But she was so persistent and so pathetic in her prayer that he yielded at last. After providing for her comfort at one of the hotels, he left by the first stage for Lillooet the day before the court opened.

Mr. Stephenson had an opportunity of seeing the Chief Justice for the first time as he took his seat on the bench to preside at the assize. Arrayed in wig and gown he presented a majestic appearance. He was far above the average height, being six feet four in his socks. His figure was as straight as an arrow. His features, when in repose, were stern and somewhat forbidding; his brown eyes were expressive and thoughtful; his hair was then just turning from black to grey; and his face was adorned with carefully-trimmed moustache and whiskers. His bearing was that of a judge who under any and all circumstances would discharge his duty as he understood it.

This was the man who, by the sheer force of his iron will and overpowering intellect, swept all before him. A giant among pigmies, he subdued the most turbulent ruffians who ever afflicted a new country with their presence. The mere mention of his name terrified hundreds who had set at defiance the laws and rulers of their own land. As the judge took his seat on that morning, a stillness as of death fell upon the crowded room. Men seemed afraid to breathe, so great was the awe which the majestic presence inspired.

The judge charged the grand jury in words of flaming eloquence, in which he depicted the enormity of the offence with which the prisoner, Robert Armitage, was charged. A human life had been taken for the purpose of robbery, and the blood of an innocent man cried for vengeance upon his slayer. One of the culprits had met a merited fate, having lost his life while fleeing from the bloodhounds of the law. The other was in the hands of the officers of the Crown, and against him an indictment had been framed and would be laid before their body. It was their duty to consider the indictment, "and," he added, with a menac-

Above: B.C.'s famous frontier judge, Sir Matthew Baillie Begbie, sentenced Armitage to the gallows.

Top right: Magistrate A.C. Elliott who knew Armitage's family history but kept his knowledge a secret. In 1876 Mr. Elliott became Premier of B.C.

Below: Lillooet in 1863 when Armitage became the first man hanged in the community.

ing look that seemed to say, "Throw out the bill at your peril." The jurors were not long in returning a true bill for murder against the prisoner. The man was sentenced, without further comment, to die and was removed from the dock.

A few days later Stephenson sought and obtained an interview with the doomed man. As he entered the cell unannounced, the prisoner, who was seated at a table, arose and, addressing his visitor, said:

"It is a long time since we met, Mr. Stephenson — at least since you were aware of my presence. I have seen you frequently, but you did not recognize me. When your cabin was robbed, I was there, and could have killed you, had I wished to do so. But you had been good to me, and I only dealt you a light tap. We thought that your gold was between the mattresses, and we only intended to take one-half. But, as you know, we got nothing." He paused, and yawned, as if he was bored, and wished to shorten the interview.

Stephenson, who was disgusted at the man's indifference, standing as he did on the threshold of the other world, contented himself with handing him the letter from his wife. Armitage opened and read it carefully and without emotion. He then crumpled it in his hand and, turning to his visitor, said:

"I owe you an apology for treating you as I did, and for my indifference now. My wife writes me that you have been more than good to her. Continue to be her friend, for she is a good sort, and was never bad. To support me and furnish me with money to enable me to "buck" at faro, she became a hurdy-gurdy girl. I always attended her to and from the hall, and, although appearances are against her, she is as pure as refined gold. Tell her that it is best that I should die, and that she will be well rid of me, in this world and the next. Tell her that when I am gone, perhaps her friends in the Old Country, who are rich and influential, will relent. All I ask is that my father and mother shall never hear of the way I died. My father turned me from his door because of something wrong that I had done, and bade me never to cross his path again.

"I married the sweet girl who calls me her husband under false pretenses. My name is neither Storm nor Armitage. I have been a sham ever since I can remember. I ought to have killed myself ten years ago, but I hadn't the courage. I was starving when I assisted in waylaying those men and in sandbagging you. But that is no excuse for the crime. I am about to die. Gambling has been my curse and has brought about my ruin. Now, my friend, say that you forgive me for my treatment of you and say goodbye.

"I commit my poor wife to your care, and if I thought God

would answer the prayer of such a wretch as I am, I would ask Him to bless you both. As it is, I can only hope that He will. I have told Mr. Elliott, the magistrate, everything — my name and my father's name. I have given him my signet-ring, and some other little things to forward to my father. Mr. Elliott will write that a horse threw me and broke my neck. He has pledged himself to preserve my secret, and I know that he will keep the pledge. Goodbye, Mr. Stephenson — forever."

Stephenson extended his hand, which the wretched criminal grasped, and pressed to his heart. It was the only time that he had shown any emotion since the commission of the murder. Stephenson assured him of his full forgiveness and, promising to care for his wife, left him to his reflections. Upon the date set he was hanged, ascending the scaffold with firmness, declining to say anything. He died without a struggle.

Mr. Elliott, who subsequently became Premier, lived for twenty-five years after the execution of Armitage. The only thing he would ever say about him was that his family were among the highest in the kingdom, and dated their descent from William the Conqueror. I was once told that it was more than suspected that the criminal was closely related to a duke, but Mr. Elliott would neither confirm nor deny that statement.

And what became of Mrs. Storm and her benefactor will be asked? I wish I could reply that they were married and lived happily ever afterwards, as the story books say. All that I do know is that about five years after the tragic events which I have recorded, William Stephenson led a lady to the altar of Grace Church, at San Francisco, where they were made one. I never saw the marriage notice. It is a strange coincidence, however, that in the next number of the San Francisco city directory the name of Mrs. Ella Storm did not appear, while that of William Stephenson did.

A Queer Character

Not to be outshone by larger centers, the fledgling community of Victoria appointed a town crier — but not for long.

I propose to relate a few of the pranks of a noted character who flourished in the Colony of Vancouver Island in the early days of the gold discoveries. His name was Butts, or Butt, as he persisted in being called. Butt was an English-Australian. He came first under my notice in 1856. I was engaged on a San Francisco newspaper at the time, and Butt was a sort of carry-all between the politicians and the editorial rooms of the *Sun*, then a leading journal. Later on, Butt was charged with complicity in the murder of James King, an editor, by one James Casey. This murder gave rise to the Vigilance Committee, and I saw four murderers hanged in the streets of San Francisco by the Vigilantes. Butt, who was imprisoned by the Committee, was later released and, in July 1858, I met him in Victoria.

He had been appointed town-crier and, equipped with a huge bell, was paid to stand on street corners, then few in number, and proclaim auction sales, theatrical performances and social events. Sometimes the government availed themselves of his stentorian voice and loud-mouthed bell to make public their proclamations and orders. This he did under the instructions of the magistrate. He was told to always conclude the reading of the proclamations with the invocation, "God Save the Queen."

As long as the magistrate was within earshot Butt adhered religiously to the instruction. But once around the corner he would cry the information, and finish by calling out "God Save (a pause of a few seconds) John Butt." For this act of disloyalty he was deposed as town-crier, and was never after employed officially.

From "crying" Butt took to scavengering. Procuring a horse and cart, he would load up on Government Street and drive around the corner of Yates Street. Then, having previously raised the tail-board a few inches, by the time he had proceeded two hundred yards the mud and filth he had gathered on Government Street would ooze out and deposit itself on Yates Street. He would then return for other loads, and dispose of them as before. Having succeeded in cleaning Government Street, he would take a contract for carting away the mud he had deposited on Yates Street, whereupon he would cart it back to Government Street, and so on, until his tactics were discovered, and he was forbidden to be town scavenger any more.

He next resorted to petty thieving, and when unconsidered trifles were scarce he would eke out his existence by begging at back doors for food and clothing. The food he would eat or throw away, according to his necessities; the clothing he would sell. Butt possessed a nice tenor voice. He had been a negro minstrel in California before he sank so low as to become a politician. One of his favorite methods to excite attention and sympathy was to knock at a door and ask for the lady of the house. Upon her appearance, he would doff his hat, assume the attitude of a troubadour and, placing his hand on his heart, sweetly warble a popular song.

The song and attitute almost invariably captured the lady's heart, and the response was a generous one.

From thieving and begging to selling whiskey to Indians was only a step, and Butt soon found himself in the chain-gang. When arraigned before the magistrate he, on one occasion, put up a plea for mercy, and recited a part of a hymn in support of the plea, but he got six months' "hard" all the same. The day following his sentence, word came from the prison that John Butt during the night had had a paralytic stroke.

Below the knees there was no feeling. He was so lame he couldn't walk a step or work a stroke. He was examined by the surgeons. Needles and pins were forced into his legs below the knees, without causing a quiver. Above the knee a pin or needle point inserted would make him howl with pain. Every method was adopted to ascertain if he was malingering. But no use, and he was finally carried to the hospital.

There for several weeks he was an object of general sympathy, and cakes, tarts, cigars and an occasional bottle of Hudson's Bay rum found their way to him. His helpless condition excited the commiseration of the other inmates. Every fine day he was carried from his room to the front of the building, and there, seated in an armchair, would bask in the sun and hold conversations with the visitors and inmates. But one day a wonderful thing happened, although Butt's wouldn't agree it was wonderful. While seated in his easy chair he was observed to slyly move one of his disabled legs. Presently he was seen to move the other. Word was sent to the physician of the hospital. By his direction several buckets of cold water were secretly conveyed to a verandah overlooking the spot where Butt sat, and emptied on his head. At the fall of the first bucketful the shock caused him to spring to his feet. Upon the third or fourth application he ran off like a deer, never stopping until he had reached town and stowed himself away in one of his many haunts.

One stormy night a missionary meeting was convened at the Methodist church. The late John Jessop presided, and introduced an Irish doctor as mover of the first resolution. The doctor ascended the platform and was observed to look anxiously about for some object. At last he exclaimed: "I wish I had a dhrop of wather." There were no taps in those days, and the necessity of water to assuage the thirst of speakers had been overlooked. Instantly rose from the fringe of the crowd near the door the fat and ragged figure of the irrepressible and ubiquitous Butt.

"Wait a minute, doctor, and I'll bring you a drink," he shouted, saying which he started for the door. Just around the corner there stood on Government Street a bar known as the Elephant and Castle. Into this bar Butt burst with a wild whoop. Seizing a gallon measure filled with water, he made off with it. The loungers started a cry that the church was on fire. While some ran to ring the bell, others poured into the church in time to see Butt amble up the center aisle and deposit on the chairman's table the dripping measure, amid roars of laughter, in which the minister and the chairman heartily joined.

About this time a scandal was created at a tea meeting at the Colonial Hotel. The dining room had been secured for tea-meeting purposes by one of the religious denominations represented here, and the kitchen was taken possession of by the ladies who prepared the tea and coffee for the regalement of the guests. John Butt was bribed to offer his services to the ladies as assistant in the kitchen. While officiating about the range, the wretch contrived to introduce into the tea kettles the contents of two bottles of Hennessy brandy.

The effect upon some of the tea drinkers — many of them rigid temperance workers — may be imagined, and I will not describe it. The next morning the scandalous affair was the talk of the town. Everyone denounced the act as a mean outrage and De Courcy, in the dual capacity of gentleman and J.P., was most pronounced in his denunciation of the perpetrators.

"I would give a pound to know the rascal," said he to a group of friends on the street.

"Major, if I tell you his name, will you give me the pound?" asked Butt, who was passing and overheard the offer.

"Yes, willingly," replied De Courcy.

"Well," said Butt, "I did it. Give me the pound."

In an instant De Courcy had him by the collar, turned him quickly around, and administered one after the other in quick succession a series of the most awful kicks. You might have heard them across Government Street so loud and resounding were they. The major had been generously provided with big feet and wore heavy brogans. Butt writhed and howled in agony. When he was at last released with a final kick that raised him off his feet and deposited him in the street, he ran off as fast as his condition would permit. He never called on the Major for the pound. If he had, I fear he would not have got it, for De Courcy was desperately hard up. But if he did not get a pound, he at least got a pounding.

There is one thing Butt did about this time that deserves mention here. A movement for the annexation of the Colony to the United States was instituted in 1866. Butt suddenly became intensely loyal. He erected a miniature gallows on Wharf Street, from which he used to turn off the annexationists, naming each "traitor" as the drop fell. I have often thought that his burlesque execution business did as much to check the disloyal sentiment as the opposition the *Colonist* paper offered to the agitation, which was at one time influential.

History relates that Rome was saved by the cackling of geese. The cackle of a solitary goose which Butt had stolen from a backyard proved his undoing. He carried the bird beneath his Inverness cape, and was met by a constable who, remarking his bulky appearance, bade him halt.

"What have you there?" he asked, pointing to the bunchy protuberance.

"It's some old clothes I'm takin' to a poor woman down in the alley," replied Butt.

The constable eyed him suspiciously for a moment, but suffered him to pass on. The culprit was making rapid tracks for his cabin when there arose from beneath his coat the most dismal squawking that ever the tongue of a goose gave utterance to. The constable seized both man and goose, and the next day the magistrate sentenced him to the chain-gang for a long term. A few weeks later the Governor pardoned Butt. He was shipped on a lumber vessel bound for Australia, and Victoria knew him no more.

Lost in the Mountains on Christmas Day

A four-mile hike for their Christmas dinner became almost a snowy grave for the four men.

The holiday season of 1858 found the people of the Fraser River town of Yale ill-prepared to face the rigors of a severe winter. Cold weather, which had set in unusually early, found many of the inhabitants still living in tents, and few occupied dwellings that were comfortable, or storm and frost defying. The lower river was closed by a sharp frost on the first day of December, and communication with the outer world, except to those who chose to risk their lives by walking over the ice, was suspended. Supplies were scarce and expensive, and long before Christmas Day arrived people began to talk dismally of the prospects of a famine in the prime necessaries.

When the day before Christmas dawned, the absence of the wherewithal for a seasonable dinner was seriously discussed. There was no poultry in town, but at Hedges' wayside house, some four miles up the Little Canyon, it was known that there were a small flock of hens and two geese that had been specially fattened for the festive occasion. It was more in a spirit of adventure than anything else that four of us young fellows — Lambert, Talbot, Nixon and myself — proposed to tramp over the mountain trail to Hedges' and purchase half-a-dozen of his birds for our tables. We started about two o'clock on the day before Christmas.

The snow, which was about two feet deep on the townsite, gradually increased in depth as we ascended the trail, until we reached the summit, where the snow was three feet, rendering locomotion exceedingly difficult. It took us till six o'clock to

161

reach Hedges', a trip that was usually made in one and one-half hours. We were completely exhausted when we came in sight of the smoke from the rude chimney, and saw the welcome glare of a light in the window as a beacon for belated travellers. A great fire of logs blazed on the spacious hearth, emitting a glare and warmth that were especially pleasant to the half-frozen poultry purchasers from Yale. A few drops of oh-be-joyful, followed by a bountiful repast of pork and beans, warmed over for our entertainment, put all in an excellent humor. Although the wind raged without, and the windows rattled, and the snow was piled in great drifts against the building, the scene within was animated and cheerful.

Gathered at the home of Hedges were several miners who had that day come in over the upper Fraser. They reported severe cold and heavy snowfall all along the line of the river. They had experienced great hardships in the walk down from Spuzzum. Several had abandoned their small stocks of provisions that they packed on their backs. In one or two instances even blankets and cooking utensils had been throw away in the anxiety of the wayworn and half-dead men to reach a place of shelter.

All these, together with our contingent from Yale, were gathered about the blazing hearth on that Christmas Eve, speculating on the chances for reaching Yale on the morrow. The landlord declared that it would be a physical impossibility for any person to pass up or down the river until the storm had abated, but we Yaleites did not agree with him. We told him that we had promised to return to Yale by noon on Christmas Day with some of his fowls, and that we intended to start in the morning for home.

I had a suspicion that Hedges, in discouraging our leaving, was anxious to retain us as guests until he had milked us of our last coin. He offered to sell five fowls and one goose at $4 apiece. We closed with the offer, and the birds were duly slaughtered and became our property. In the morning the storm still raged. The cold was intense. The building was almost buried in snow which lay three feet on the level at the river brink. This meant four feet on the summit, and enormous drifts everywhere.

In spite of these obstacles we four foolish young men proposed to start for home with the birds after an early breakfast. Several old and experienced miners remonstrated with us, but in vain. We were determined to go. One grey-haired prospector likened us to a lot of silly geese. Another said we ought to be sent to an asylum for idiots to have our heads examined. Another produced a tapeline, and with a solemn expression on his grim face proceeded to measure us.

"What for?" asked one of our party.

"I'm a carpenter out of a job," he said. "I shall begin to make four coffins the moment you pass out of sight, so that when you are brought back stiff and stark, there will be nice, comfortable shells to put you in. Bill here (pointing to his mate) will proceed to dig four graves as soon as the storm is over."

We all laughed heartily, and entreaties were futile. We discarded all advice, shouldered the poultry, and proceeded to pick our way up the mountain side, intending to follow a zig-zag trail. The snow was indeed deep, and as we advanced it grew deeper. We broke our way through several heaps fully six feet high. The wind howled dismally through the trees and underbrush, scooping up as it swept by great armfuls of snow, and piling it in fantastic shapes and drifts on all sides.

Before we were well out of sight of the cabin the trail had vanished. Every landmark by which, under other circumstances, it might have been regained was gone, too. I looked at my watch. We had started at eight o'clock, and it was now eleven. We had not made, according to my calculation, a mile. Besides, we had no compass and, being off the trail, it was impossible to tell whether we were going north or south. We floundered on through the snow, which grew deeper and deeper as we ascended the mountain. Sometimes one of the party would step into a hole and disappear for a few moments. We would all stop, and, having hauled him out, would press on again in the hope of again recovering the lost trail. The cold grew sharper and the wind fiercer.

There was one fur coat in the party. The wearer of it, young Talbot, who was not at all robust, seemed to feel the cold more keenly than the rest of us. Several times he paused as if unable to go on, but we rallied him and chafed him and coaxed him, until he was glad to proceed. Another hour passed in the senseless effort to overcome the relentless forces of nature. By that time we were four as completely used up and penitent men as ever tried to scale a mountain in the midst of a howling snowstorm, with the thermometer standing at zero. Talbot at last sank in a drift, panting for breath and weeping from exhaustion. We dug him out with our hands. He tried to rise, but his strength was spent.

"Boys," he moaned, as he sank down again, "I am done. I can go no further. Leave me here. My furs may keep me warm until you can get help; but, at any rate, save yourselves if you can. I am not afraid to die, but I would rather not die on Christmas Day with my boots on."

"Fiddlesticks!" cried I. "What nonsense to talk of dying. We are all right. Only make another effort and we'll be at the summit. After that it will be all down hill and dead easy."

Talbot shook his head sadly, and continued, "Promise me you won't let me die with my boots on." Tears sprang from his eyes, and froze on his cheeks. He lay helpless and inanimate in the snow.

Lambert and Nixon were strong and sturdy young men and as brave as lions, but they were greatly disheartened at the condition of our wretched companion. Besides, like me, they suffered severely from the cold, which had grown more intense as we proceeded. All wished that we had listened to the people at the inn. But it was too late now for regrets — there was only room for action. Something must be done quickly or all would perish. We divested ourselves of our packs, casting the fowls from us as if we hoped never to see another goose or chicken as long as we might live. The fowl sank in the new-fallen snow. We saw them no more, and with them disappeared the wherewithal for a grand Christmas dinner which we were taking to our friends at Yale.

While we deliberated as to the best course to pursue, for it was as difficult to retrace our steps as it was to proceed, a sudden cry from Lambert attracted my attention. Pointing to Talbot, he exclaimed, "He has fallen asleep! Wake him up, in God's name, or he'll freeze to death!"

We seized Talbot and stood him on his feet. He was limp and helpless, and fell over again. His eyes were half-closed, and his breathing was so faint that when I put my face against his lips I could scarcely detect the slightest evidence that life still abode in that tired body. We rubbed his face, hands and ears with snow. Lambert and Nixon called him by name and begged him to speak. We pounded him on the back and stood him up again. Although he began to show faint signs of awakening, he was so far gone that he could not raise foot or finger to help himself.

While this was going on I hurriedly broke a few dead limbs from a pine. Clearing the snow from the roots of an upturned tree, and with the aid of a knife, with which I made some kindling, soon had a small fire burning. To this fire we hurried Talbot.

By dint of rubbing and pounding, and the assistance of a few drops of a cordial commonly known as H.B. Company rum, Talbot shortly revived. He shook off his desire to slumber, but he was very weak, and kept calling on his mother, who was thousands of miles away. The exertion we put forth to restore Talbot had set us aglow. We resolved to keep the fire up and remain under the shelter of the fallen tree until the storm abated.

"By Jove," said Lambert, "why didn't we think of it before? If we had kept those chickens we might have had a rousing Christmas dinner after all. We might have cooked them at this fire."

But it was too late. We searched, but could not find the first feather. So we tightened our belts, consulted our flasks and tobacco pouches, and sat down by the fire. Talbot, having become rested by this time, showed no signs of falling asleep, but he was very weak and despondent.

About two o'clock the snow ceased to fall. The wind gradually fell from a roaring blast to a gentle zephyr, and then died away altogether. Towards the south, the sky, which for two or three days had presented a hard, steely aspect, seemed to darken. Presently great heavy masses of clouds stole slowly along the eastern horizon, the cold lessened, and the temperature rose rapidly. Then we knew that a Chinook wind had set in, that the back of the cold weather was broken, and that if we could but regain the lost trail we should be saved!

I rose from my place near the fire, and proceeded to reconnoitre. I floundered along for a short distance, but not a vestige of the trail or the tracks we had left in our painful progress was visible. It was now four o'clock in the afternoon. We had been out eight hours, and night was coming on rapidly. I began to fear that we were little nearer our goal than when we started. I saw no other prospect than being obliged to remain where we were all night.

I tightened my belt another hole, and was in the act of retracing my steps, when a sound that fell upon my ears sent a thrill of joy through my tired and aching frame. "Is it the ring of a woodman's axe echoing through the canyon?" I asked myself.

I listened intently, and soon my doubting heart supplied the answer. It was only the beat of a woodpecker's bill on the hollow trunk of a tree. I turned away with a feeling of heartsickness at the prospect of passing the night without food or shelter. My mind was filled with apprehension lest the delicate constitution of Talbot should succumb to the exposure. As I prepared to return to the fire another and more familiar sound reached me. My heart almost stood still as I paused to listen.

Then there broke full upon my ear the deep bay of a dog! It rolled up from the valley, and reverberated through the rocky depths, disturbing the awful stillness of the forest, and imparting to me hope and confidence at the prospect of a rescue. I drew my revolver from my belt and fired five charges. I listened to the reports as they echoed through the forest and died away in the distance. Then — oh! thrice welcome sound! Never in all my life did a human voice seem so sweet in my ears as that which I heard utter almost at my feet: "Coo-ee! Coo-ee!"

I must have "Coo-eed-d" in response, because again I heard clear and full and distinct a man's voice, as he shouted: "Where are ye, boys?"

"Here," I cried, "this way."

In another moment a great mastiff broke through an enormous drift and barked loudly as if to encourage us. Talbot rose to his feet in his excitement and tried to call, but his voice died away, and he could not utter a word. He tried again and again, until his vocal chords at last limbered up. He managed to burst the bonds of silence that his excitement had imposed upon him, and emitted a long, resonant: "Coo-ee! — Coo-ee!"

We shouted again and again. Soon from the foot of the mountain there came back the answering call of many voices. The mastiff leaped as if with gratification at having found us, and led the way down the mountain side. We plunged through snow that reached to our armpits, following the dog. In a short time we came in sight of a large cabin with smoke curling from an ample chimney. As we approached a number of men came out to greet us. I paused to look and rubbed my eyes.

"Is this a dream? Where are we, anyhow? No, it cannot be. This is not Hedges', surely?" I asked of one of the men, as we drew near.

"That's just what it is, sonny," replied the man.

Hedges advanced and offered me his great fat hand. "I didn't expect to see you silly boys alive again," he said, "and I ought to have tied you up before I let you go out in the storm. Come in, anyhow, and have something, and then join us in our Christmas dinner, which is just about ready. You must be hungry."

The "carpenter out of a job" scanned us closely from head to foot, and then said, "Well, I'll be durned. It's just my luck. I'm out $50 on your coffins."

Everyone laughed at this, but few besides ourselves understood how nearly our obstinacy and self-conceit had brought us to the "narrow home."

So we went inside, and accepted the landlord's "something." About five o'clock we sat down to a roast of fowl and goose, and spent a jolly evening. Two days later we reached Yale, where we had been given up for lost.

But the best of the tale remains to be told. It was ascertained by Hedges, who saw where we had made our fire. He reported to our friends in town, much to our annoyance and confusion, that in all our wanderings and flounderings we had never been more than an eighth of a mile from the inn, having walked around in a circle after we lost the trail!

The Pork-Pie Hat

The author records an incident in which "Gassy" Jack Deighton, the founder of Vancouver, learns that not only sheep can be fleeced.

You want me to tell you something about Burrard Inlet in the early days. Well, although I can tell you a good deal, I did not get here until 1865, when Stamp put up the Hastings Mill, but the first sawmill was built by Hicks & Graham in 1863. The first white men who settled on the site of Vancouver were John Morton, William Hailstone and Sam Brighouse. About Christmas, 1862, they located 550 acres, and when the government came to survey the land it was sold to them at $1 per acre. Morton and Brighouse afterwards divided their land, which lay west of Burrard Street and took in English Bay, by tossing a coin — head or tail.

I was employed as a hand logger at that time. Most of the hands at the mills were Americans and Indians. The little village which sprang up near the Hastings Mill was called Granville. Deighton's hotel was the only place of entertainment. Its owner was called Gassy Jack, for the reason that he was such a gas-bag, always talking and blowing. After a while people got to calling the place Gastown, after Jack. He used to keep his money in a "safe," as he called it. In reality it was a cigar box such as holds a hundred cheap cigars. This "safe" used to rest on a shelf back of the bar during the day, and at night Jack would lock it up in a drawer and go to bed. No such thing as a robbery ever entered his head. He was honest himself, and imagined every one else was the same.

At the time of which I am speaking I worked at Hastings Mill. I was on the day shift, and one evening — it was at the close of a beautiful day, warm, clear and still — I came up to the hotel from my work. I was tired and hungry, and began taking a swift wash in a tin basin that stood on a packing case near the hotel door. Half a dozen other hungry men were waiting their turn to wash and dry themselves upon the one towel, when I heard the clattering of horses' hoofs on the hard road. Looking up I saw two Indian ponies, on which were seated a gentleman and a lady. The gentleman was dressed in a suit of dark clothes that looked worn and dusty. He was light complexioned, and his hair, which was parted in the middle, was streaked with grey. He wore a long, heavy, tawny moustache which swept across his face and almost lost itself in his ears. I remember I thought that but for the hairy ornament he would be quite good-looking.

The lady seemed to be about eighteen. She had the loveliest black eyes, large and lustrous, and fringed with the longest lashes that you ever saw. She had on a dark-green riding-habit, and on her jet-black hair was perched a little turban of a style then much worn, and known as the "pork-pie." She had a sweet, engaging face, and sat her horse gracefully.

The man dismounted, and assisted his companion to alight. She leaped down, with the skirt of her riding-habit gathered in her hand. After taking in the crowd with a quick glance of her glorious eyes, she busied herself with beating her habit with a riding-whip, sending up little clouds of dust from the folds.

"Gentlemen," exclaimed the man, in a soft and pleasant voice, as he removed his hat, "good evening."

"Good evenin'," returned one of the boys.

"Kindly direct me to the landlord," said the new arrival.

"You will find him at the bar mixin' lickers," said the spokesman.

At that moment Gassy Jack appeared at the door. Seeing the gentleman and the beautiful lady, he removed his hat and bowed almost to the ground, for he was awfully soft on the woman question.

"You are the landlord, I presume," said the gentleman.

"I ham," replied Jack.

"Well, my daughter and I have ridden over from New Westminster, and she is very tired. Can we get two rooms, with supper tonight and breakfast in the morning?"

"Sure!" cried Jack, in his most effusive manner. "Yer can have the best the house has got, and what it hasn't got I can get yer."

"We heard," said the gentleman, "that there is a vacancy here in the school-teaching line. As my daughter is a teacher we thought we would cross and look at the surroundings before applying for the place. We like the appearance of things. My name is Crompton — Lionel Crompton — and my daughter is Miss Crompton."

"By gracious!" said Jack, striking his fat thigh with his hand.

"She had a sweet engaging face and sat her horse gracefully."

"It's just what we want — a schoolmarm — and I'm a trustee, and I'll help your gal git the job."

"Thanks, awfully," returned Mr. Crompton. "We'll stay here overnight, and perhaps two or three days longer. Kindly have our horses looked after."

Jack summoned the Indian hostler, and the animals were led off to the stable. While this conversation was in progress Miss Crompton continued to dust her habit, occasionally raising her pretty eyes to survey the group that stood spellbound by her beauty.

"Come, daughter," said Mr. Crompton, "we will remain here." Giving her his arm, he conducted her to the parlor, as Jack called his best room. The parlor was small and low-ceilinged. Its walls were adorned with cheap pictures of uproarious color and design, and a card bearing the legend, "God bless our home." There were two or three books, among which was a hymnal, for Jack allowed church services to be held there on Sundays. In one corner was a piano with a few sheets of music lying upon it.

The girl laid down the whip, removed her "pork-pie," and went to the piano. After running her fingers over the keys she began to play, and, oh! the music that she brought out. It swept through the house in a great gust of melody and, floating outside, filled the woods with delicious sounds. It was a great treat, in the midst of that wildwood, to hear such strains. Presently she sang in a clear and strong contralto several popular airs. The boys who were gathered at the door clapped and whooped and shouted for more. Some who were due on the nightshift at Hastings wanted to stay and listen all night.

As father and daughter passed into the dining room, we regular boarders sheepishly followed and took our seats on either side of the table. The evening meal never amounted to much. The food was generally wholesome enough, but on that occasion it was rich. Pork and beans were not in evidence for a wonder, and there was cold chicken on the list, and Jack, who could not take his eyes off the beautiful vision, waited on the pair in person and saw that they wanted for nothing.

We boys supped high that night, and when the meal was over and the party had gathered on the verandah, Deighton passed around the cigars. As daylight faded the girl returned to the parlor and again attacked the piano, to our intense delight. In the meantime a few of the boarders managed to pluck up courage and spoke to her, and found her affable, but very prudent and sedate.

Some one in a burst of enthusiasm proposed a dance, with Indian girls as partners. The young lady said she did not play dance music, and dancing was sinful; besides, it was bedtime and she would retire. Wishing all a sweet goodnight, she again swept the group with a glance from her expressive eyes. Then she kissed her papa and, gathering up her long skirts with the remark, "Don't be late, dear, and don't drink any more," she walked towards the stairs.

There were two coal-oil lamps burning on the table, and I seized one and volunteered to light the girl to her room. She thanked me and I led the way to the door. Then she said: "May I ask your name?"

"Certainly," I replied. "My name's Simmons — Bill Simmons."

She laid a little hand on my arm and looked long and searchingly into my eyes. I trembled like a leaf on a tree. The floor seemed to be giving 'way beneath my feet. All things were in a whirl and my knees just knocked together. In my excitement I almost dropped the lamp. How I refrained from falling at her feet and telling her that I loved her, I cannot say. Perhaps I did — I don't know — I was so upset. In a few seconds I recovered myself, and then I saw that her sweet eyes were filled with tears. In broken accents she said:

"Oh, Mr. Bill — Simmons, I mean — can I trust you?"

"You can," I remarked. "Hope I may die if you can't." I drew a cross on my chest with my finger as a mark of fidelity.

"Oh! my poor, dear father," she moaned.

"What's the matter with your old man — I mean your daddy?" I asked.

The poor thing just leaned her head on my arm and her body shook with emotion, while I trembled and felt like sinking through the floor. I wanted to put an arm about her, and tell her that she was dearer to me than life, but I couldn't. She held one arm, and the other was occupied with the lamp. At last she said:

"How can I tell you? But I must. My father is addicted to drink. When he gets among a lot of nice, handsome young fellows like you and Jack he never knows when to stop. I want you to promise me that when you go downstairs again you will do all in your power to get him to bed."

"All right," I said. "I'll do it."

The dear girl murmured her thanks and, resting her hand again upon my sleeve, gave my arm such a squeeze that the blood seemed to leave my heart and fly to my head. Again everything seemed to give 'way. My head went round and round like the great flywheel at the mill. A buzzing sound, as of a circular saw ripping through a plank, filled my ears. At this critical moment the girl released my arm and opened the chamber door. Then I recovered myself and said, in faltering tones: "Don't thank me — you are quite welcome."

The first building in what is today Vancouver was the Globe Saloon, built in September 1867 by an ex-sternwheel steamer captain called Jack Deighton, opposite. Jack is shown on the roof, after unfurling the Union Jack which "...had been his chum for 40 years." Because of his talkative nature, he was nicknamed "Gassy" Jack and the community which grew up around his saloon was called Gastown. Later it became Granville, then Vancouver. Deighton died when he was only 45. A newspaper commented that he was "...an original in his way, and his name became almost a household word with most of our citizens."

Again she murmured her thanks, again she placed her hand on my arm, and again the hot blood flowed like a current of electricity through my veins. The door stood open behind her. She gave me another long, searching look, and then, quick as thought, she sprang backwards and slammed the door in my face! Then the key was turned in the lock. I found myself standing alone on the threshold. I pulled myself together with difficulty, and tumbled, rather than walked, down the stairs. In the bar I found the strange gentleman "shouting for the house," as they say in Australia, or "standing treat," as British Columbians put it. All hands lined up at the bar, and Jack, who was very much "on," insisted upon toasting the strangers.

"'Ere's to the new boarders!" he shouted, "'specially to the young 'un. Her father's a dandy, but she's a peach."

The toast was drunk with cheers. The health of the old 'un was next washed down the parched throats of the millmen and loggers. Then Jack got his share of toasting, and before midnight all wobbled on their legs. The old gentleman had to be assisted to his room, where he was put to bed with his boots on. While we were tucking him in the covering he knocked on the partition of his daughter's room and called out:

"Alish — Alish, dear (hic), are you all right?"

"Yes, papa."

"And (hic) are you very, very comfor'ble?"

"Yes, papa."

"Then goodnight, my sweetheart, pl-pleasant dreams to you, may good digestion wait on appetite (hic)."

"Oh, fie, papa!" cried the girl.

"Yesh, dear (hic), what ish it?"

"You've been drinking again. Oh my! What will poor mamma say?"

"Shay? Why, she'll shay, 'I'm a jolly good feller, which nobody can deny.' Goodnight."

Alice, apparently disgusted with her father's condition and incoherency, made no reply, and he presently turned over and went to sleep. Then the house fell into a deep slumber, broken only by the snoring of the inmates as they slept off their heavy potations.

The morning broke brightly. The sun was high in the heavens, and the little birds in the woods had breakfasted and were caroling their thanks, when the Indian hostler, who had joined in the revelry, awoke from his drunken stupor and proceeded towards the stable to look after the horses. He stopped at a spring to cool his parched throat, and then dragged his aching head and unwilling limbs to the barn. He opened the door and peered into the stalls. To his surprise, they were empty! Where

In 1870 the town of Granville was surveyed, with Gassy Jack's saloon in the middle of an intersection at Carrall and Water Streets. Gassy promptly bought a corner lot, moved his saloon and enlarged it into Deighton House. In 1874 he advertised that it offered "...comfortable parlours and commodious single and double bedrooms." The men at left are sitting on the verandah.

he had led and bedded two ponies the night before there was a void. Scarcely trusting his eyes at first he stood open-mouthed, gazing into the untenanted stalls.

Then, uttering one word "Clattawahed" (Gone), he rushed to the hotel, and woke up Jack. He in turn, ran to the stable and then back to the house. He ascended the stairs two steps at a time and knocked at the old man's room, gently at first. But meeting with no response he gave a thundering bang and shouted, "Beggin' your parding, Mr. Crompton, but your horses is stolen."

Still no reply. Then Jack turned the door handle and slowly pushed his red face into the room. The bedclothes were tumbled and the room was in disorder. The window was wide open, but the gentleman, like his ponies, was gone!

Jack flew to the room to which the girl had been conducted. He tapped gently, then a little harder. Still meeting with no response, he softly opened the door. The blind was closely drawn, and the light in the room was uncertain. But he could discern the beautiful black hair which he had admired so much the evening before straggling over the pillow. What struck him as most singular, resting on what seemed to be her head, was the pork-pie hat!

"Strike me lucky," he shouted. "I'm jiggered if the gal hasn't gone to bed with her hat on for a nightcap! Miss," said he, "wake up! Your daddy's gone, and the horses is stolen."

There was no answer. With an air of becoming modesty, Jack tiptoed into the room and advanced to the side of the bed before

he discovered that there was no girl there! She, too, had gone, leaving behind her a wig and a hat. On a chair was spread her dark-green riding-habit. Jack beat his head with his clenched fist. Bounding downstairs to the bar he ran straight to the drawer in which he nightly deposited the "safe." The drawer had been pried open and the "safe" was gone, too.

"Robbed, done up, buncoed, ruined!" he wailed.

"There was $400 dollars, nearly, in that 'ere safe, and that man and that girl is the thieves."

A hue and cry was raised, and a party was soon on the trail of the supposed robbers. A short distance away were found eight gunny sacks that had been tied about the horses' feet to muffle the sound of their tramping as they were led past the hotel. Near the same spot the "safe," rifled of its contents, was picked up. The pursuers reached New Westminster quickly, but the robbers had got away by crossing to the American side and reaching Washington Territory.

It was afterwards learned that they were male members of a strolling theatrical company. Learning of Jack's careless habit with money, they had disguised themselves for the purpose of robbing his "safe." The fellow who acted the part of the girl and captivated the lumbermen was one of the most expert impersonators of female characters on the Coast. They were never caught.

As for "Gassy" Jack, he bought a real safe, donated the pork-pie hat to an Indian chief's wife, and committed the wig to the flames.

The Lions

After thirty years the Cariboo miner returned to the community of Gastown, to discover in its place a thriving city called Vancouver.

The day had been one of the most beautiful of a mild and delightful winter. On the Pacific Coast there had been neither ice nor snow, high winds nor heavy falls of rain. Throughout the length and breadth of British Columbia railways and wagon roads had been unobstructed, and open-air industries were prosecuted without a moment's cessation.

The inhabitants revelled in the warm sunshine, tender flowers bloomed in the gardens, buds on the trees burst with fullness, birds carolled on every bush, crocuses and violets raised their pretty heads, and fields were verdant with young grass. It was, therefore, with a feeling of deep sympathy that the people of the province read in the daily despatches from the East dismal stories of deep snows and intense cold; of entire families being frozen to death in their homes; of railway trains stalled for many days in great drifts; of fierce blizzards that scattered misery and starvation and death in their paths; and of destructive conflagrations that could scarcely be quenched because water in the pipes was frozen solid.

The day, as I have noted, had been bright and beautiful and the sun had sunk to rest behind the Lions. These wonderful carvings from the workshop of Nature challenge the admiration and excite in all beholders a feeling of awe, as high up in the mountain at the entrance to Burrard Inlet they crouch like huge sentinels, keeping watch and ward over the gateway through which is destined to pass the commerce of our mighty Empire.

As the sun went down and its dying beams gave the Lions a goodnight kiss, the full moon arose in majesty and splendor. Casting its rays on the massive images, it clothed them in a white

From near or afar their snow-capped splendor dominate the skyline. The majestic Lions have reigned over Vancouver's harbour as silent sentries since time began.

garb of matchless beauty. A brief while before, gold with a rich setting of red and blue had captivated the senses. Now there was a wonderful transformation — gold had turned to silver, and the vivid coloring had fled, giving place to a dark background of sky, from the depths of which sparkled and glinted innumerable stars like diamonds reposing in a gigantic tiara. As the moon advanced on its course its light fell on the cresting of the tiny waves in the harbour that had been fanned into action by a gentle breeze, and imparted a rich, phosphorescent glow to the moving waters.

In the light of the moon on that evening a stranger stood upon one of the wharves of the city of Vancouver. He was tall and spare, with a swarthy complextion. His hair was streaked with grey, and he looked like one who had worked hard and lived hard, for his hands were calloused with toil and his face was furrowed with deep lines of care and exposure. He gazed with rapture upon the lovely scene, and as he paced up and down he conversed audibly with himself. At intervals he addressed the Lions as though they were sentient beings and could divine his words. He paused often, as though he expected a reply. For the twentieth time he asked the sentries: "How long have you been on guard?"

A voice at his elbow responded, "About two hours."

The man started and trembled. He turned quickly, and saw standing at his side a tall young man with smooth face and long, light hair. He was of athletic build and in his hand carried a heavy walking stick.

"Who the devil are you and what are you doing here?" demanded the startled stranger, with a threatening gesture.

"I am the watchman on this wharf, and it is my duty to ask, 'Who the devil are you and what you are doing here?' Strangers are not allowed to loiter here after dark. You needn't be so cheeky, either."

"I wasn't speaking to you," the man said, after a pause.

"Well, who were you speaking to, then? There were none but you and me here."

"I was talking to myself," replied the man.

The young fellow gazed into the depths of the other's face long and searchingly before he replied. His inspection was apparently satisfactory, for he presently said:

"I guess you wouldn't set these sheds afire? Or rob them? Or waylay anyone, would you? You're the right sort, I think; but I fear you're a bit dotty. Now, ain't you — just a little bit gone up here?" he asked coaxingly, as he tapped his own forehead with his finger.

"Do you mean crazy?" asked the stranger.

"Yes," replied the watchman. "When a man goes along talking to himself and asking all sorts of fool questions in the dark of nobody, the police run him in, and sometimes he is sent to Westminster for treatment. I am not sure but I had better take you in charge as a vagrant."

"If you do, my friend," returned the man, "you will have your trouble for your pains. I am not mad and I am not a vagrant, as this wad will show." He produced from a hip pocket a good-sized roll of bank bills, which he held before the watchman's eyes.

"I am as sane as you. I am a miner just down from Cariboo, where I have lived and mined for thirty years without once coming to the Coast. I have saved a few thousand, and I came here to blow part of them in with friends whom I used to log and run with years ago. I have been here two days, and I'm blessed if I have yet found a man or woman whom I knew when I was last here.

"Now I find myself liable to be run in as a lunatic or vagrant by a man who must have been in short clothes when I went away. Funny, isn't it? Everything is changed — everything save the magnificent harbour, the mountains and the wonderful animals. They're the only things that have not altered."

The watchman again looked hard at the stranger, and waited until he resumed.

"Yes, I knew this place when it was marked Granville on the map, but its common name was Gastown, after Gassy Jack Deighton, who was a good old soul, if he was rough and raw, and did have a tongue that was never still. There were about two dozen mean little shacks in Granville when I went away, and the inhabitants numbered only about fifty. All over this townsite were forests of great trees and tangled underbrush. These have passed away, and I find in their places a busy city of forty-five thousand people.

Where I left narrow trails and logging roads I find paved streets with sewerage, and on every side handsome business and residential structures. Where I groped my way with a lantern my path is lighted by electricity. Where I climbed hills with difficulty I now ride in a street car. Where I drank from a slimy well there is now a full supply of pure water. Where there was only a muddy beach and a few ships at the mills there are now miles of wharves at which lie the argosies of every nation discharging or taking on cargo. Where there was not a railway in any part of the province, I find this city the terminus of two great transcontinental systems whose trains arrive and depart every hour of the twenty-four. But I weary you." remarked the man.

"No, no," responded the watchman. "On the contrary, you

interest me. Go on, please."

"Granville and Gastown exist no longer save as memories. You call the big town that has brushed the others aside and sprung up upon their site, Vancouver. I have walked the streets and ridden in the street cars until I am tired, and found, as I have said, none whom I knew. I am going back to the mines. Before starting, I thought I would come down this evening to the waterside to — to — talk awhile with the — the — animals."

"The animals?" queried the watchman. "What animals do you mean? There are no animals here that I can see, excepting you and me. What do you mean? Are you getting off your nut again?"

"Young man," said the other, with an air of solemnity," cast

Vancouver was incorporated in April 1886 with its population of 2500 clustered in Granville and the waterfront quarter of Gastown. At Deighton House, Gassy Jack still held court and any wounds inflicted by a scoundrel in a pork-pie hat were long since healed. The new city was barely two months old on June 13 when life for both pioneers and newcomers alike changed dramatically. That day the winds rose and

your eyes upward to the summit of yon mountain and you will see two majestic lions bathing in the moonlight. I watched them when the sun was going down, and now I see them arrayed in robes of silvery brightness and matchless beauty. They are just as they were thirty years — aye, thousands of years ago. They are as unchangeable as the laws of our Maker. When I speak of animals I mean those lions."

"Do they answer you when you talk to them?" asked the young man, with a mischievous smile.

"No, but it's mighty comfortable to think that they would if they could.

"How I'd like to hear them roar! You have everything here to make a big city. You have a grand harbour, commodious

tragedy unfolded as fire swept through the townsite. By day's end, 22 people were dead and Gastown was obliterated. Granville lay in ashes but the next day pioneer spirit prevailed and construction of a great new city began. The ensuing frenzy of construction and the arrival of the Canadian Pacific Railway while the grounds still smouldered both exemplified human resilience and provided a legacy for the future.

business premises, hotels, schools, churches, overland and street railways, sewerage, water cheap and abundant, good streets and a lovely park. You live at a fortunate time, young man. Just think of it: In 1873 Henry Edmonds held a sale of Government lots in the Granville townsite. The highest bid he could get for a lot was $100, and he only sold six. Those very lots are held now at $20,000 each, and a lot on Hastings Street, for which no one would bid in 1873, has recently been disposed of for $41,000.

"The street noises, the cars, the cabs, and the delivery vans and carriages, the rush and crush of business and the throngs of people confuse and deafen me. They drive me almost mad. I sigh for the solitude of the hills and valleys of golden Cariboo, and there I shall go to spend the balance of my years, while you will grow and prosper with the town. Now, tell me some of the great things that have occurred since I went away."

"Well," began the watchman, "I was very little when my parents came to reside at Granville. Of course, there was a good deal of talk of a railway coming in. But as the years slipped along many people who had settled on the Inlet got discouraged and left. But others came in and took their places, and the town began to grow slowly. Then the railway was built to Port Moody, and a struggle began between Granville and Port Moody over which would be the terminus. While this struggle was going on a terrible thing happened.

"On the 13th of June, 1886, I was playing with my brother on the road near where Cambie and Cordova Streets come together. Lots were being cleared and brush fires were burning. Suddenly a high wind sprang up and smoke and flames were carried directly towards the lightly-constructed buildings. The atmosphere grew so hot I could scarcely breath, and a dense cloud of smoke swept along Water Street. Someone cried, 'Fire!' and there was a rush of people towards the spot where we boys were playing.

"Then I saw a great tongue of flame shoot out of the cloud of smoke and cast itself like a fiery monster upon a small wooden hotel that stood in its way. In an instant it seemed as if the hotel was in flames from cellar to attic. The guests fled, barely escaping with their lives, leaving all their effects behind them. We boys were paralyzed with fear, and stood looking at the fire as it swept towards us, until a man dragged us away. Then we began to cry. Men were shouting and women wailing and shrieking. Some who tried to save their goods had to abandon them, for both sides of the street were now in flames. Others who lingered too long in their houses were burned to death.

"We never saw our home again, for it was one of the first to go with everything in, except the family, who saved themselves by flight. The hungry flames swept on, the frenzied inhabitants fleeing before them. In less than three hours the townsite was swept almost clean, and, worse than the loss of property, there had been a lamentable loss of life. Thirteen bodies, many of them burned beyond recognition, were found on the streets or among the dying embers. Three men who had sought refuge in a store were burned to a crisp. A mother and her young son, whose retreat was cut off, descended into a well, and when the flames passed by both were found dead. They had been suffocated by smoke and heat. There were many narrow escapes, and the calamity would have paralyzed most communities.

"But not so here. At four o'clock the next morning, while the ashes of their buildings were still glowing, Pat Carey and Duncan Macpherson began to rebuild. Others followed their example. Relief was sent from all quarters, and under the stimulating influence of Mayor McLean and an energetic board of aldermen, the town soon recovered itself.

"After the fire the battle for the terminus was renewed, and raged fiercely for some months. Then one day the Port Moody people were plunged into a state of deep despair by the announcement that the railway would be extended to Granville. The residents here were elated. Granville was then a straggling village of about two hundred buildings and twelve hundred inhabitants. The first train reached here in May 1887, and you can be sure that there was great rejoicing, and town lots went up with a bound. The name of the town was changed to Vancouver, and people began to flock in and buy property and build. And so things have gone on ever since, until the city has reached its present size, and it is growing faster now than ever before."

The moon had sunk behind the distant hills and a chill wind swept over the sleeping city. The stranger rose from his seat. He said that he was tired and would seek his couch, for tomorrow he must start back for his claim. "Besides," he added, "the Lions have drawn the curtains of night about them and gone to bed. So I, too, shall say goodnight and goodbye."

The next day and the next, the watchman, cursing his stupidity in not having asked the stranger's name, searched the hotels and boarding-houses in vain for a trace of him. But he was gone and had left no sign.

The Lions remain faithful to their trust. Day following day finds them grim, watchful and incorruptible, presiding in silent majesty over the western gateway of the Dominion. And so will they continue to guard countless generations of men, as they come and go, until heaven and earth shall be rolled up like a scroll, and there will be no more sea.

Happy Tom

When the author gave the cheerful young man the nickname "Happy Tom," he little realized the tragedy that would unfurl.

The morning was bright and warm. I had risen early and, after a dip in an eddy in front of Yale, was slowly picking my way along the bar towards a trail that led to the bench where the principal business houses were located. Then I saw approaching a tall youth of perhaps eighteen. He leaped from boulder to boulder as he advanced, seeming to scorn the narrow path which led around the rocks.

He was active enough for a circus acrobat, I thought, as I paused to watch his agile movements. As we neared each other the young man began to whistle, pouring forth the most melodious sounds. The airs he selected were from songs that were popular at the time, and the execution was so exquisite and harmonious that I paused to listen so that I might draw in every note. When he found that he was observed the youth ceased to warble, and, dropping from a boulder on which he was perched to the ground, bashfully awaited my approach.

"Good morning," I said. "You must have struck it rich — you seem so happy."

"No," he replied, "I haven't struck it rich. On the contrary, I have found nothing."

"Then why do you whistle?" I asked.

"Oh, because it makes the time pass pleasantly. Besides, I never let trouble bother me — I shed it like a duck sheds water from its back. I can't imagine how any man can be unhappy so long as he walks straight and acts right. I don't mean to do anything wrong in all my life, and if I don't have good luck I'm never going to fret."

"That's the proper spirit," I said. "Stick to that and you'll come out all right. What's your name?"

"Tom," he said, with a funny look in his eyes.

"Tom — Tom what?" I persisted.

"No, not Tom Watt — just Tom — that's all."

"But surely you have another name?"

He shook his head with a light laugh as he said, "My name's only Tom in this country. Call me that and I'll always answer.

"No," I said; "I'll call you Happy Tom. Your philosophy is sound and good and your face shows that you have a light and happy heart."

He laughed again and passed on down the bar. As he went along I saw that his clothes were ragged and his boots in holes. A week elapsed before I met the boy again. He then walked along the main street warbling a popular tune with an energy and skill that were marvellous. He filled the air with melody and people ran to their doors to listen to the sweet sounds. Tom was certainly a charming performer, and it was not long before he became a popular favorite. No party or dance was complete without Tom and his remarkable whistle. He was an exemplary young man. He would neither drink liquor nor smoke. He was witty without being coarse, rude or offensive. "Swear words" were strangers to his lips, and honesty of purpose and kindly thought shone from the depths of his clear eyes and lighted up his ingenuous countenance.

I had many conversations with him and found him very intelligent. His uniform good nature was magnetic, and he grew upon me so that I soon got to like him very much. When I left the river in 1860, one of the last hands that I enclosed in a goodbye grasp was Happy Tom's, for the name had stuck to him. His eyes glistened as he approached the side of the canoe and wished me good luck.

"Tom, old boy," I exclaimed, "adhere to your principles and you'll be one of the foremost men of the Colony. You've got it in you. Give it a chance to get out. Don't drown it with bad whiskey or kill it with worse company."

The happy fellow began to whistle an operatic air. Then he switched off upon "Home, Sweet Home." As my frail canoe plunged into the foaming current and began to glide swiftly down stream he sent after me "Cheer, Boys, Cheer." When I looked back just as the canoe began to turn the first bend in the river he was perched on a huge boulder, still pouring forth his happy soul in sweet and far-reaching melody.

If any one should have then predicted that when Happy Tom and I next met it would be under circumstances of a most awful and soul-terrifying character I would have called him a false prophet or a fool. Yet it so turned out, as the sequel will show.

In the summer of 1872 there arrived at Victoria from England a young lady named Ellen Forman. She was the daughter of Alderman Harry Forman, a resident of James Bay. She bore a high certificate as an English public school teacher, and was pretty, as well as talented. John Jessop was then Superintendent of Education, and the young lady was not long in securing a school at a fair salary, where she gave entire satisfaction. About this time her father married again and the couple with the young school teacher went to reside at Mr. Forman's house, a one-story affair containing six rooms and a kitchen. About this time exciting news came of the discovery of a supposed rich vein of silver ore near the town of Hope. Silver was then worth $1.10 an ounce and the shareholders in the new discovery were each rated in public estimation as worth at least a million dollars. Among the owners in the mine were George Dunbar, Sewell Moody, Wm. Sutton and Thomas Chooley. These men were regarded as far and away the richest men in British Columbia. A test shipment of ore to San Francisco yielded $208 to the ton, and it was reported that there were many thousand tons of as rich rock in sight.

The owners I have named came to Victoria one day to sell shares, which they had no difficulty in doing. Alderman Forman and the visitors were thrown much together, and Forman invited Chooley to his house and introduced him to his daughter. The father was dazzled by the reputed wealth of the mine owner, and the young girl, perhaps, was anxious to lay aside her books and exchange the little, unpretentious dwelling for a palace with servants and fine clothes and diamonds galore.

It was a case of love at first sight. Chooley was at least twenty years older than Ellen Forman. He was strong and stout and masterful in his way, while she was pretty and petite and shrinking in her manner. But as love is said to delight in contrarieties, the difference in age, habits and dispositions proved no obstacles to an early union.

In a few weeks the two were married amid the blare of trumpets, the glare of Chinese lanterns and the popping of champagne corks. All predicted a brilliant and happy career for the pair. They were treated and toasted and feasted, and if old shoes and showers of rice could ensure happiness, Mr. and Mrs. Thomas Chooley ought to have been the happiest pair of mortals on earth. Among the presents was a solid silver tea set made of metal from the Fort Hope mine. They went from here to San Francisco, where they put up at a leading hotel.

While there a serious quarrel occurred, due to the bridegroom's unjustifiable jealousy. He asserted that his wife did not love him. The idea was absurd and unjust. They returned to

Tom Chooley and his beautiful wife on their wedding day.

Victoria, and in due course a child was born at Forman's house where the pair resided. The coming of the child produced no change in Chooley. He treated his pretty wife with distrust and cruelty. When Forman remonstrated with him, Chooley drew a revolver and threatened to shoot him. He was restrained and left the house, taking rooms at the Driard Hotel. In a few days a peace was arranged and the Chooleys went back to the Forman house.

About this time it began to be rumored that the mine was not as rich as had been supposed. The vein had been probed, was found wanting in high-grade rock and showed signs of "petering out." It was also observed that Chooley's wealth, which was believed to be inexhaustible when he was married, had taken unto itself wings and flown away to the realm of unprofitable investments. As his means vanished, Chooley became more brutal to his wife and abusive to her parents.

Instead of the baby exerting a softening influence, it made him harder. The sorrowful little wife was patient and strove bravely to mellow the fierce and wicked disposition of the man whom she had married. He repelled all overtures. It was even said that he beat her on more than one occasion, and that he and Forman had come to blows in consequence. The parties continued to inhabit the little house where Chooley, who had now begun to drink heavily, terrified all by his wild threats and beastly language and actions. Tragically, his threats were not all wild.

The evening of January 22, 1874, was dark and dismal. Several inches of snow had fallen during the day and walking was most unpleasant. About 6:30 in the evening I was standing in front of my office when Richard Brodrick, a well-known coal merchant, approached, saying:

"As I came across James Bay bridge just now I met Dr. Powell and Dr. Davie walking rapidly towards the Government Buildings. They told me Harry Forman had been shot."

"By whom?" I asked.

"They did not tell me," replied Brodrick.

A few minutes' quick run brought me to Forman's house. I knocked at the door. There was no response. I turned the handle — the door was locked. I ran round to the kitchen and tried that door. It was locked, too. I endeavored to raise a window, but all was fast. As I passed round to the open front door again two policemen, Clarke and Beecher, came up. From them I got the information that Chooley had shot Forman and that the wounded man had fled to the house of James R. Anderson, on the opposite side of the street, where he lay dying. Chooley, they added, had barricaded himself in Forman's house and was heavily armed.

The police kicked in the front door and were met with two or three pistol shots fired in quick succession. The constables retreated, and Chooley appeared at the opening, pistol in hand. After fastening the door he again disappeared. The police surrounded the house and proposed to wait for daylight before renewing the assault.

I walked to the Anderson house, and there lay Harry Forman on a lounge. Every breath that he drew caused the warm blood to surge upward through a wound in his side. He had been shot through the left lung and was making a dying deposition.

In substance, he said that when he came home to dinner at six o'clock that evening Chooley was roaring drunk. He had taken possession of the dining room, and a cocked revolver lay on the table by his side, while a demijohn of liquor stood on the floor. He refused to allow the table to be set in the dining room. For peace sake Mrs. Forman laid the cloth in the kitchen. Forman, his wife, and Mrs. Chooley, with her wee one on her knee, sat down to dinner. They were conversing in an undertone about the best course to be pursued under the distressing circumstances when Chooley suddenly appeared.

With a fearful oath he aimed the weapon at Forman who was in the act of conveying food to his mouth. The ball passed through Forman's hand. The wounded man with a cry of agony rose to fly, but the wretch fired again, the ball this time passing through Forman's body. As the women and Forman ran from the room Chooley fired once again, the ball passing through a loose fold of the baby's blanket, making a hole, but doing no further injury. The whole party found shelter at Mr. Anderson's, where Forman died the following morning.

I returned to the Forman house after having heard the deplorable story and found the police still inactive and disposed to await the coming of day before resuming operations. Indeed, the militia had been sent for to form a cordon about the house. At this moment a little Englishman named W.H. Kay volunteered to enter the house and secure the murderer if a window could be pried. After several efforts the kitchen window was raised and Kay's small figure vaulted through the opening into the dark apartment.

He found the dining room door closed but not locked. Gently pushing the door open, he encountered an obstacle. The obstacle proved to be Chooley's body, for he was lying dead drunk across the doorway. Kay required but little space through which to squeeze his small frame, and once inside he leaped on the murderer with a yell and held him until the police entered and secured him.

Chooley was brought to trial. He was followed to and from

The Eureka Mine in the 1870s. It was an ill-fated venture. Two of its shareholders, S.P. Moody and F. Garesche, drowned in the *Pacific* disaster, while Tom Chooley became one of nine men hanged at Bastion Square Jail, below. The building is today Victoria's Maritime Museum.

the scene of trial by an angry multitude who sympathized with the wretched family. His lawyer was insulted while on his way from court on the first day of trial, and threatened with bodily injury, so intense was the feeling. The jury was not long in deliberating and when a verdict of guilty was rendered the spectators were transported with delight. Mr. Justice Gray passed sentence of death, which was to be inflicted six weeks later. Chooley took his sentence with calmness. His only defence was that he had been tricked into marriage and that his wife had been untrue to him.

Three days before the day on which Chooley was to die, I was admitted to the death cell. I found the man calm, but fully impressed with the idea that he had been wronged by Forman, who knew the state of his daughter's heart. I reasoned with him without avail. His one absorbing thought was that he had acted within his rights in committing the murder — that he was merely an instrument to punish Forman. He told the same story and expressed the same belief to his clergyman, whose ministrations he readily received and in which he expressed belief. As I was leaving I casually remarked that I once resided at Yale.

"Yes," he said. "I knew you there."

"Do you know," I answered, "that I have been told by a hundred different persons that you were there in my time, and yet I cannot recall your features."

His eyes rested on the floor for a moment as if he were in deep thought. Then he raised them to mine and said. "Are you quite sure that you never met me on Fraser River?"

"Quite," I replied.

Again he seemed to drop into deep thought. Then he rose to his feet. The setting sun shone through the little grated window that furnished air and light to the cell, and a golden beam danced like a sprite along the white-washed wall. The doomed man raised a hand as if he wished to grasp the fleeting ray. When he turned towards me again his eyes were filled with tears.

"And you don't remember me?" he said, sorrowfully.

"No, I cannot recall a line of your face."

"Perhaps this will aid your memory," he said. Then from his lips there issued a stream of delightful notes.

I leaped to my feet, surprised and overcome by the revelation that the music conveyed.

"Good heavens!" I cried. "You don't mean to say that you are — you are — 'Happy Tom?'"

"The same," said he. "Happy no longer but the most dejected and miserable wretch on the whole of our Maker's footstool! Fifteen years ago I was the merriest and happiest man in the colony. Today I am a miserable felon and am about to die. After you left Yale I fell into bad company and took to drinking and gambling, and here I am at last — the natural end of all such fools. Had I been sober I would never have married that woman, and there would have been no murder."

He paused and burst into tears. In the midst of his grief I asked him if he would withdraw his words about his wife.

"No," he fiercely shouted. "I withdraw nothing."

At this moment one of the guards informed me that my time was up. As I extended my hand the convict said: "Mr. Higgins I have one request to make of you. Will you come and see me hanged on Friday?"

"No!" I replied. "Ask anything else and I will grant it; but not that — not that!"

"It's my last request — I insist," he urged.

"Oh! I cannot," I replied.

"What?" he said, caressingly, "you will not come and see poor Happy Tom — the boy you christened in the long ago — die like a man! Come, say you will. I shall never ask anything more of you."

I yielded at last. On an early spring morning, when Nature had recovered from her long winter sleep and the song birds had mated and nested and were bursting their throats with songs of gladness, and the sun had just peered above the eastern rim of the globe, as if to witness the gruesome proceeding in the old jail yard at Victoria, they led Thomas Chooley to be hanged by the neck until he was dead.

As he crossed the yard to the scaffold his frame showed not the slightest tremor, his face wore its natural hue. As he advanced his eyes wandered over the group of officials and spectators until they encountered mine. A smile of recognition flitted across his face. Then it seemed as if the intervening years were rolled away. He and I were suddenly transported to the waterfront at Yale and he had just told me his name was only Tom, and I had named him "Happy Tom."

He ascended the scaffold with a firm step and listened unmoved to the reading of the death warrant and the prayers of the good man who stood at his elbow. His legs were then tied, a cap was drawn over his face and a bolt was sprung. The next instant all that remained on earth of Unhappy Tom Chooley was a writhing body suspended between heaven and earth.